BASIS FOR BUSINESS B1
WORKBOOK

SIMON CAMPBELL

ADVISER
MICHELLE HUNTER, GRAFENAU

Cornelsen

Basis for Business B1
Workbook

Im Auftrag des Verlages erarbeitet von	Simon Campbell, Dortmund
Beratende Mitarbeit	Michelle Hunter, Grafenau
Redaktion	Anna Batrla
Redaktionelle Mitarbeit	Martin Maier, Katrina Walsh
Bildredaktion	Uta Hübner
Projektleitung	Murdo MacPhail
Umschlaggestaltung	hawemannundmosch, bureau für konzeption und gestaltung, Berlin
Layout und technische Umsetzung	Sabine Theuring, Berlin
Illustrationen	Andreas Terglane, Kassel
Cover:	© Mauritius Images, Pixtal

Bildquellen
S. 6 © shutterstock, StockLite; S. 8 © iStockphoto, Michael DeLeon; S. 9 © shutterstock, kanvag; S. 10 © iStockphoto, AVAVA; S. 12 © fotolia, iofoto; S. 13 © iStockphoto, Neustockimages; S. 15 © shutterstock, auremar, © iStockphoto, Pali Rao; S. 18 © shutterstock, AISPIX; S. 20 © iStockphoto, Rainer Plendl; S. 25 © iStockphoto, Pali Rao; S. 29 © iStockphoto, mediaphotos, © shutterstock, Yuri Arcurs; S. 33 © shutterstock, Dariusz Gudowicz; S. 36 © iStockphoto, Andrey Tsidvintsev; S. 39 © iStockphoto, Anna Khomulo; S. 42 © iStockphoto, Jacob Wackerhausen; S. 48 © iStockphoto, gilaxia; S. 50 © iStockphoto, Sjoerd van der Wal; S. 55 © shutterstock, auremar, Rob Wilson; S. 63 © Alamy, Westend61 GmbH

Weitere Kursmaterialien
Coursebook mit Audio-CDs und Phrasebook   ISBN 978-3-06-521005-8
Teaching Guide mit Toolbox CD-ROM   ISBN 978-3-06-521007-2

www.cornelsen.de

1. Auflage, 5. Druck 2020

© 2012 Cornelsen Verlag, Berlin
© 2018 Cornelsen Verlag GmbH, Berlin

Das Werk und seine Teile sind urheberrechtlich geschützt.
Jede Nutzung in anderen als den gesetzlich zugelassenen Fällen bedarf der vorherigen schriftlichen Einwilligung des Verlages. Hinweis zu §§ 60a, 60b UrhG: Weder das Werk noch seine Teile dürfen ohne eine solche Einwilligung an Schulen oder in Unterrichts- und Lehrmedien (§ 60b Abs. 3 UrhG) vervielfältigt, insbesondere kopiert oder eingescannt, verbreitet oder in ein Netzwerk eingestellt oder sonst öffentlich zugänglich gemacht oder wiedergegeben werden.
Dies gilt auch für Intranets von Schulen.

Druck: H. Heenemann, Berlin

ISBN 978-3-06-521006-5

PEFC zertifiziert
Dieses Produkt stammt aus nachhaltig bewirtschafteten Wäldern und kontrollierten Quellen.
www.pefc.de
PEFC/04-31-1156

Table of contents

Unit			Page
1	**First impressions**	• talking about responsibilities and current projects • describing companies and products • giving contact details • introducing yourself and your company	5
2	**Then & now**	• talking about your job experience and your past • talking about skills and abilities • making telephone calls	11
3	**A company tour**	• welcoming visitors and socializing • talking about rules and regulations • describing a process • writing emails • developing small talk tactics	17
4	**Big plans**	• talking about plans and projects • looking at graphs and sales figures • practising taking part in a meeting • placing an order	23
5	**It's a deal**	• discussing terms and negotiating a deal • talking about differences • comparing prices and terms	29
6	**Changing times**	• talking about experiences • discussing and making arrangements • updating a diary • writing emails to make and change appointments	35
7	**Out of the office**	• talking about recent activities and new developments • practising small talk and saying goodbye • making polite complaints • listening for information in presentations	41
8	**At a trade fair**	• describing features and benefits of products • distinguishing formal and informal emails • reading a report	47
9	**Culture matters**	• talking about a company's history • making conversation at a restaurant • making and dealing with complaints	53
10	**Smooth operations**	• talking about supply chains • discussing hypothetical situations and consequences • talking about future training plans	59
	Progress checks		65
	Answer key (exercises and progress checks)		71
	Transcripts		81

Preface

Das **Basis for Business B1** Workbook hilft Ihnen, Ihre Englischkenntnisse selbstständig zu erweitern. Durch das handliche Pocket-Format kann Sie das Workbook überall begleiten: Auf dem Weg zur Arbeit, auf Geschäftsreisen, in einer Kaffeepause oder am Schreibtisch.

Die abwechslungsreichen Übungen im Workbook erweitern und vertiefen die im Kursbuch **Basis for Business B1** behandelten Themen und Strukturen. Das Workbook kann dabei sowohl zum Selbststudium zu Hause als auch im Unterricht verwendet werden.

Das **Basis for Business B1** Workbook ist in zehn Units unterteilt, die auf das Kursbuch abgestimmt sind. Sie enthalten:
- Übungen zu den wichtigsten Grammatikstrukturen und zum Wortschatz
- Over to you-Übungen, um das Gelernte zu personalisieren
- sprachliche Tipps und Did you know?-Kästen mit ergänzenden Informationen zum Thema der Unit
- 3 Progress checks zur Selbsteinschätzung und Überprüfung der Lernfortschritte (im Anhang)
- Hörverständnisübungen in jeder Unit (Audio-CD)
- vollständige Transkripte und Lösungen (im Anhang)

Wir wünschen Ihnen mit dem **Basis for Business B1** Workbook viel Spaß und Erfolg!

First impressions

1 Which department is responsible for each of the activities shown in the pictures below?

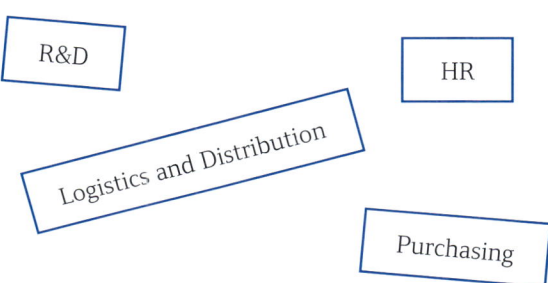

R&D

HR

Logistics and Distribution

Purchasing

Unit checklist
- talking about responsibilities and current projects
- describing companies and products
- giving contact details
- introducing yourself and your company

2 Choose the correct verb form to complete the dialogue: simple present or present continuous.

Roger: What does your department do / is your department doing¹ exactly?
Jane: We're responsible for training staff. We normally organize / are organizing² seminars for employees, but there are training programmes for management too. At the moment, we look / are looking³ at some new ones which staff could find interesting.
Roger: Right. Is there anything in particular?
Jane: Well, currently we speak / are speaking⁴ to another training organization which prepares / is preparing⁵ some new concepts.
Roger: Do you think / Are you thinking⁶ they can offer you anything?
Jane: We don't know / are not knowing⁷. A colleague of mine works / is working⁸ on this now. She can tell you more about it.

3 Listen to this interview between Roger and Jürgen. Are these statements true (t) or false (f)? Correct the false statements.

1   New projects can last two to three months.
2   Only project teams decide on the objectives.
3   The seminars on time management are only at Logan's headquarters.
4   Jemma Thompson is working on a project with a new supplier in France.
5   The subject of Jemma's report is about working hours.
6   Jemma's time management is chaotic.
7   Purchasers can have time off work thanks to flexitime.
8   Logan tells suppliers to reduce their prices.

> **Tip** Die Begriffe 'buyer' oder 'purchaser' können als Übersetzungen für das Wort „Käufer" verwendet werden. Einige Firmen bevorzugen den Ausdruck 'procurement manager', um die Funktion dieser Mitarbeiter zu beschreiben.

4 Complete this email sent from a head of department to his employees with the correct words or expression from the box.

administration • manufacture • developments • send • coordinating • put • sell • supply

From: Mike Harvey
To: Team Harvey

Dear all,
Today I'd like to discuss some of the recent changes in our company.
Firstly, we're introducing a lot of IT ....¹ which should make processes better with our suppliers when they ....² the equipment we order. We try to ....³ our products to our retail outlets on time, but this is still difficult. The good news is that we are able to ....⁴ our products more quickly now at our factories around the country.
Secondly, our CEO plans to ....⁵ a number of departments together into one unit, and people from different departments are currently working on this project. The idea is difficult to ....⁶ to some employees as it means a lot of change. Mark represents our department in this project team. He is ....⁷ the project; he has to make sure that the times for meetings are OK with everyone. There's also the idea to make payroll ....⁸ the same throughout our subsidiaries in Europe.
As soon as I have more news on any of the projects, I'll give you an update.
Best wishes,
Mike

5 Which words go together? Complete the sentences below by adding the most suitable word from the box.

department • company • employee • rep • range • facilities

1 The parent ...., which owns this subsidiary, is based in Edinburgh.
2 We manufacture our products in five production .... in the US.
3 Our customer care .... always looks after our clients.
4 Each sales .... is responsible for selling in his or her own area.
5 This picture of our product .... shows everything we sell from soft drinks to beer.
6 All workers are paid at the end of the month through a system of .... reimbursement.

6 Match these board-level positions with the statements below. What does each term stand for?

CFO CEO CTO CIO COO CRO

1 ......: He is the director of the board.
2 ......: He is a member of the board responsible for financial planning.
3 ......: Her role in the board is to manage the use of computer software.
4 ......: She is the board member responsible for analysing and managing her firm's day-to-day business and activities.
5 ......: His task at board level is to analyse the dangers to future business.
6 ......: One of her tasks at board level is to look after R&D activities.

7 Listen to the description of a company structure. Fill in the missing information.

Board of Directors: Jane Seymour ....¹ (position)			
John Brown ....² (position) Department active in ...., ... and ....³	Richard Blake ....⁴ (position) Responsible for .... and ....⁵ staff	Anna Lenoir ....⁶ (position) Department based in ....⁷	Linda Crolla ....⁸ (position) Responsible for four ....⁹

8 Unit **1** First impressions

8 Think about your company and its products or services. What does it offer and what are your responsibilities?   *over to you*

....
....
....
....
....
....

9 Complete this description of the company Lasco Energy using the correct form of the verbs in brackets (simple present or simple present passive).

```
Lasco Energy
http://www.lasco-energy.com/                    Q- www.lasco-energy
```

Lasco Energy ....¹ (produce) electricity and gas for the Scandinavian market, and we ....² (base) near Oslo. The company ....³ (divide) into six business units which ....⁴ (include) Production and Marketing. Electricity and gas ....⁵ (sell) from our stations to private and industrial customers who ....⁶ (locate) all over Norway and Sweden. We also have some subsidiaries in other countries, so we are quite active in Europe. Sometimes, when Lasco ....⁷ (build) new power stations, engineers ....⁸ (send) from our headquarters to these locations.

Did you know?

Der Anteil von Frauen in Führungspositionen in Europa ist 2011 gestiegen. Frankreich verzeichnet einen Anstieg auf ca. 20%. Als erstes Land weltweit hat Norwegen 2003 eine Quote von 40% weiblicher Mitglieder in den Aufsichtsräten von börsennotierten Unternehmen eingeführt.

**10 Listen to this telephone message.
    Write down the details.**

Notes

Name: ....¹

Hotel: ....²

New director: ....³

Tel: ....⁴

Website: ....⁵

11 Rearrange the words to make questions.

1 is/Who/Steven Jones/for/message/leaving a/?

....

2 at/staying/Which/Steven/hotel/is/?

....

3 would/like/What/to/Steven/do/?

....

4 Ann/Where/find/can/new/the/website/?

....

12 Practise your telephoning skills. How would you express the following statements?

1 Wofür sind Sie zuständig?

2 Wie schreibt man das?

3 Könnten Sie das bitte wiederholen?

4 Leider habe ich Sie akustisch nicht verstanden.

5 Ich hoffe, ich störe Sie nicht?

Then & now

2

1 An applicant explains how he got his job.
Put his statements in the right order.

Unit checklist
- talking about your job experience and your past
- talking about skills and abilities
- making telephone calls

- **a** At the end of the interview, they told me they would make a decision soon.
- **b** Based on my application, I was then invited for a job interview.
- **c** I started at the beginning of last month.
- **d** First, I wrote an application including my CV and sent it to the company.
- **e** and asked me to return to their offices to sign the contract.
- **f** I received an email a few days later – they offered me the position
- **g** The HR department then read this application and decided I had the right profile.
- **h** During the interview, they asked me questions about my job experience and qualifications.

2 Complete the dialogue below using the correct form of the verbs in brackets (simple past).

Claire: What . . . . .¹ (you, do) after graduation?

Catriona: Well, on leaving university I . . . . .² (take) a course in business studies which . . . . .³ (be) at an institute in Leeds.

Claire: . . . . .⁴ (you, like) it?

Catriona: Not really, but at least I . . . . .⁵ (be able to) get a qualification in business. After that, I . . . . .⁶ (join) a retail company.

Claire: I also . . . . .⁷ (use to) work in retail, but I . . . . .⁸ (find out) that there . . . . .⁹ (be) more opportunities in IT so I . . . . .¹⁰ (decide) to go back to university to do an IT course.

Catriona: . . . . .¹¹ (you, be able to) find a job in IT after that?

Claire: Yes, but I . . . . .¹² (not, apply) for a job immediately after the course. I . . . . .¹³ (want) to spend some more time in Italy. I . . . . .¹⁴ (use to) live there.

3 Two participants, Peter Brown and Anna Wilson, are talking to each other during a break at a seminar. Listen and answer these questions.

1. Where did Peter use to work?
2. Who had communication problems?
3. What sort of company did Anna work at in Paris?
4. Why did she like working in Paris?
5. What were the problems with her former boss?
6. What kind of contract did she have?
7. Why can't Peter speak French fluently?
8. Why is his life more relaxed in Amsterdam?

> **Tip** Der Begriff 'you know …' oder 'y'know …' wird oft verwendet, um beim Gegenüber in einem Gespräch Zustimmung zu finden.

4 Read the sentences below and add the missing words to the puzzle. What is the word in column A?

1. I didn't want to go to the pub, but my colleague was able to … me so I went.
2. She graduated from university with a … in engineering.
3. We were able to … a new product on the market for the first time last year.
4. We have a … of €100,000 for marketing.
5. Because there are so many projects, she often … tasks to her assistant.
6. Our company is quite … . We always have new ideas for new products.
7. If you want the job, all you have to do is sign this … .
8. I know the problem is difficult but we must … with it.

```
        A
1  P         D
   2  D
   3  L     N
   4  B
   5  D   E
       6 I   O
   7  C
       8  D
```

12 Unit **2** Then & now

5 Listen to the speaker introduce Steffen Krenz. Complete these notes about him.

1993: .... in Munich;
    job in .... department
1998: .... of team in US,
    which .... car components
2001: returned to .... ;
    job in ....
2004: got an .... from university
2006: .... Krenz Automotive Components
2009: .... engineers
2010: ....

Did you know?

Dem europäischen Doktortitel entspricht im englischsprachigen Raum ein PhD. Wenn jemand einen Doktortitel hat, wird dieser bei der Anrede im Englischen meist nicht erwähnt. Die Anrede mit 'doctor' dient als Berufsbezeichnung für Ärzte.

6 Write down the questions to the answers below.

When did Steffen Krenz graduate from university?
Steffen Krenz graduated from university in 1993.

1 .... ?
   Steffen Krenz studied mechanical engineering.

2 .... ?
   Steffen joined BMW.

3 .... ?
   Steffen's team was based in the US.

4 .... ?
   Twenty engineers were hired.

5 .... ?
   Krenz Automotive became successful in 2009.

7 What qualifications do you have? Summarize your educational background in four or five sentences.

over to you

....
....
....
....
....
....
....

8 Match the words from the box to the words below. Then use these words to complete the sentences.

> environmentally • multinational • open-plan • paternity • public • works

.... company
.... leave
.... transport
.... friendly
.... council
.... office

1 David is on .... His wife had a baby last month.
2 I rarely go to work by car. I normally use ....
3 Our .... means we can work easily together as our desks are next to each other.
4 The employees are represented by the .... at our company.
5 I work for a ....; we have offices all over the world.
6 All our products are .... Their effect on nature is minimal.

14 Unit **2** Then & now

9 Complete the sentences with the correct form of the verbs in brackets (passive).

1 Some years ago, plane tickets could .... (buy) from a travel agent, but nowadays they can .... (purchase) online.
2 Our new computer model .... (launch) two years ago; it can .... (use) for a number of different applications.
3 Components used to .... (import) from Italy, but now they can .... (produce) at our plant in Cologne.
4 All orders used to .... (process) here in my office, but now this .... (do) by another department.

10 Paul Hillmann, a purchaser, is calling Ruth MacDonald about his order. Listen to the phone call and write down the details.

Original order:
Original delivery date:
Supplier's problem:
New delivery date:
New offer:
Future orders:

11 Read this email Paul sent to Ruth. Decide whether the statements below are true (t) or false (f). Correct the false statements.

Dear Ruth,

I'm afraid the current problem about the 1000 K9 components is not the only difficulty we have. Three weeks ago, a colleague of mine informed me that your company sent us 100 K7 devices. When they arrived here, we saw that most of them were either broken or not of the quality we expected. We contacted your company about this, but the reaction was not very positive. The faulty devices still have not been replaced.
Two days ago, I tried to arrange a meeting to discuss this and the current K9 problem with you and your team. I spoke with one of your colleagues – he didn't give me his name – but he could not arrange a time for a meeting.
I informed our head of department about these problems this morning, and we are thinking about the business relationship we have with your company. We would like to hear what you can say about this asap.

We look forward to hearing from you.

Regards,
Paul

1 The K7 devices were delivered to Paul's company.
2 They K7 devices didn't have quality problems.
3 Ruth's company was informed about the K7 problem.
4 The K7 devices were replaced by Ruth's company.
5 One of Ruth's colleagues was contacted to arrange a meeting.
6 A meeting was arranged to discuss the problems with Ruth's team.
7 Paul wants to know what Ruth can say about the current situation.

12 Practise your telephoning skills. Complete the following statements.

1 Ich würde gerne mit Frau Brown sprechen.

   I'd like to ....

2 Leider ist sie momentan nicht hier.

   Unfortunately, ...

3 Könnten Sie bitte später zurückrufen?

   Could you please .... ?

4 Danke, dass Sie zurückrufen.

   Thanks for .... my call.

A company tour   3

Unit checklist
- welcoming visitors and socializing
- talking about rules and regulations
- describing a process
- writing emails
- developing small talk tactics

1 Geoff Anderson, a buyer from the company Shoeshine, writes an email to David Wong, a sales rep working for Silver Phoenix. Choose the correct adjective or adverb (1-8) in the email below.

From: geoff.anderson@shoeshine.co.uk
To: david.wong@silverphoenix.com.hk
Subject: New shoe models

Dear David,

Thanks for sending me your new brochure recent/recently[1]. I had a thorough/thoroughly[2] look at it. The new shoe models are not high/highly[3] expensive. However, I would like to know more about your general/generally[4] conditions. I'll be in Hong Kong next week, so do you think we could meet on Friday, 11th April at 10 am? I know that you hard/hardly[5] have any time at the moment, but I would appreciate a short/shortly[6] meeting.
I also hear your new headquarters look great/greatly[7] – maybe I could have a look around? Could you please send me a quick/quickly[8] email if this time is OK with you?

Kind regards,
Geoff

2 Geoff and David meet in Hong Kong. What do they say? Match the questions to the answers.

1 Excuse me, are you David Wong from Silver Phoenix by any chance?
2 Is this your first visit to our factory?
3 Shall we start with the company tour?
4 What's that over there?
5 What were we talking about?
6 How about going to a restaurant after work?
7 What can I get you?
8 Is there anything you can recommend?

a   Actually no. I was here last year.
b   I'd like some coffee, please.
c   Sure, I'd love to try the local food.
d   That's our main sales area.
e   The fish is quite good, but I really like the steaks.
f   The German market.
g   Yes, let's do that.
h   Yes, that's me.

3 **Listen to Geoff and David's discussion. Are these statements true (t) or false (f)? Correct the false statements.**

1. ☐ Geoff had to take a taxi because his train was late.
2. ☐ Geoff could take his hand luggage into the cabin.
3. ☐ Geoff's company is thinking of increasing its orders.
4. ☐ Geoff would like to discuss delivery.
5. ☐ They agreed on a new price.
6. ☐ A consultant looked at the British shoe market.

Tip Die Frage 'How do you do?' wird häufig bei einem ersten Treffen gestellt. Sie ist keine echte Frage, sondern entspricht dem deutschen Ausdruck „Angenehm". Man antwortet darauf mit 'How do you do?' oder 'Pleased to meet you.'

4 **Do you remember what was said in exercise 3? Complete these sentences, then listen again to check.**

1. You're . . . . well.
2. . . . . your coat.
3. Anyway, ... a seat.
4. . . . . some coffee?
5. . . . . a good trip?
6. Geoff, ... Helen Li.
7. . . . . to coffee and biscuits.
8. If you don't . . . ., what exactly did you want to talk about today?

18 Unit **3** A company tour

5 Complete the sentences below with the correct form of the verbs in brackets (simple past or past continuous).

1 While we . . . . (drive) to the customer, he called to cancel the meeting.
2 I . . . . (not go) to the meeting last Monday as I had another appointment.
3 Her mobile rang while she . . . . (cross) the street.
4 While we . . . . (discuss) the problem, my colleague . . . . (interrupt) us.
5 He . . . . (not meet) his client yesterday because he . . . . (work) on a project in his office.
6 "What . . . . you . . . . (do) when the customer cancelled the contract?" "I called the sales director."
7 "What . . . . you . . . . (do) when the customer cancelled the contract?" "I was showing him our new product range."

6 Have a look at the sentences below and complete the statements with the most logical sentence (a or b).

1 I have a regular meeting with our head of department on Mondays at nine o'clock in my office, and we don't want to be disturbed.
    a   You needn't phone me at that time.   b   You mustn't phone me at that time.
2 We take safety guidelines very seriously.
    a   You must wear a helmet during our company tour.   b   You don't have to wear a helmet during our company tour.
3 This company has a no-smoking policy.
    a   You don't have to smoke.   b   You mustn't smoke.
4 These rules are for everybody.
    a   You can follow them.   b   You have to follow them.
5 This project is very important.
    a   All aspects must be considered.   b   All aspects needn't be considered.

7 Read these sentences describing the steps in car production. Then put the statements in the correct order (1-8).

- a After that, they are put together on the assembly line.
- b Every car produced is then inspected in a system of quality control.
- c Finally, they are taken from this car park and transported to cities around the country.
- d First, the components are ordered from our suppliers.
- e If any mistakes are found in a car, it is taken away for further inspection.
- f After inspection, the cars are driven from the factory and parked near to the factory for a limited period.
- g On arrival, the components are normally kept in our warehouse for a short period.
- h Then, these components are taken into the factory.

8 Anna Smith has sent you an email saying she plans to visit your company next week. Write an email to her and include these points.

- thank her for her email
- find out her exact date and time of arrival
- offer an airport pick-up
- offer to arrange hotel accommodation
- ask Anna if she would like a company tour

Did you know?

Im englischsprachigen Raum verwendet man in der Anrede beim ersten E-Mailkontakt häufig den Nachnamen. Dann geht man aber meist relativ schnell und unabhängig von Hierarchiestufen zum Vornamen über.

9 Small talk is often used in business meetings. Think about your favourite restaurant or café. What is special about it? Write a short dialogue in which you invite a business partner to go there with you.

Over to you

....
....
....
....
....
....

10 Two colleagues are discussing the business situation at their company. Complete their conversation with the correct words from the box.

> competitors • expect • changes • inspected • instruction • launch • recommendation

Fiona: As you know Peter, the ....¹ of our new car model two years ago was quite successful, but now we have a few problems with sales.

Peter: Yes, I know. I think one reason for this is that we have so many ....² in the same market. I think we need to make some ....³ to the colour and design. This could make our car more attractive to younger customers.

Fiona: Yes, you're right. Our customers also ....⁴ good quality and a good price. By the way, I hear that management gave our R&D and marketing departments the ....⁵ to form project teams to think about a possible solution.

Peter: Perhaps we should make a ....⁶ to the board that the budget for advertising should be increased?

Fiona: Yeah, maybe. But I think we should also look at quality control. Each car should be thoroughly ....⁷ for defects before it leaves the factory. The system's just not good enough at the moment.

11 Have a look at the blue words. Which words go together? Match these sentence halves.

1 Our ad
2 She's a skilled
3 We have a number of key
4 When you visit our factory, please follow the safety
5 All our protective

☐ suppliers who deliver all the components we need.
☐ guidelines because it can be quite dangerous.
☐ equipment, such as helmets, is kept in this room.
☐ agency is responsible for advertising all our products on TV.
☐ worker. She can operate all the machinery in our factory.

12 Practise your small-talk skills. How would you express the following statements? Use the words in the box below.

Have you ever … • What's … • … outdoors? • … well worth … • … do you like to play? • … local speciality.

1 Haben Sie schon einmal thailändisches Essen probiert?

2 Welche Sportarten treiben Sie gerne?

3 Verbringen Sie viel Zeit in der Natur?

4 Wie ist das Leben so in London?

5 Ich denke, dass Paris einen Besuch wert ist.

6 Ich kann diese regionale Spezialität wirklich empfehlen.

Progress check 1 → page 65

22 Unit **3** A company tour

Big plans 4

1 What are these people going to do?

Unit checklist
- talking about plans and projects
- looking at graphs and sales figures
- practising taking part in a meeting
- placing an order

He is going to eat his steak.

2 Write three sentences about what you are going to do next week.   *Over to you*

3 Read the sentences below and complete them with the correct form of the verbs in brackets (*will* future).

Helen: The last delivery of metal parts was really expensive. I hope the price ....¹ (not increase) over the next few weeks. What do you think?

John: I'm not sure. It probably ....² (not go) up, but we ....³ (have to) wait and see.

Helen: That's true, but I think we need to do something. Maybe we should contact the new supplier we found in Barcelona. I think I ....⁴ (contact) their sales department tomorrow. Hopefully, they ....⁵ (make) us a good offer.

4 Look at these graphs. Match each graph to a situation below (a–d).

a .... Sales peaked during the first half of last year.
b .... The number of employees stayed the same.
c .... At first, sales may decrease slightly, but they will probably rise again in the third quarter because of the positive market development.
d .... There was a sharp decrease in profits.

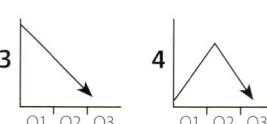

5 Listen to a sales manager talking about sales of machine tools and make notes. Then draw the graph.

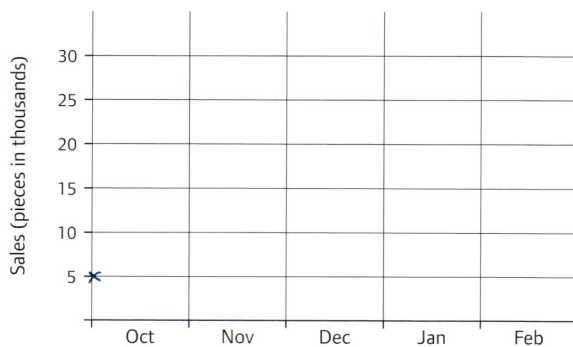

Did you know?

Es gibt verschiedene Arten von Diagrammen:
line graph — *Liniendiagramm*
pie chart — *Tortendiagramm*
bar chart — *Balkendiagramm*
table — *Tabelle*

6 Complete the sentences with the correct form of the verbs in the box (future passive).

> call • change • not inform • give • not deliver • accept • tell • train

1 OK, it's agreed. The project deadline .will be changed. to the end of March.
2 The contract .... by management next week.
3 I hope we .... about the board's decision. Our team can't work on the project without it.
4 A meeting .... to discuss the plan.
5 Where .... the staff .... to use our new IT system?
6 In her new position as team leader, she .... new tasks.
7 I'm afraid the goods .... on time. Our supplier has some transport problems at the moment.
8 This is not his project. He .... about future developments.

7 Andrew, a personnel manager from Premier Dairies, is talking to Christine, a member of the works council at the company. Listen and answer the questions below.

1 What is Andrew's plan for the staff?
2 The company is under pressure. What is the reason for this in Christine's opinion?
3 What does Andrew mean exactly by changes to work schedules?
4 What does Christine say about the staff's reaction to the plan?
5 What does Andrew say about paying the staff?
6 When will Christine inform Andrew about the staff's reaction?

Unit **4** Big plans 25

8 Do you remember what was said in exercise 7? Complete these sentences, then listen again to check.

1 Let me . . . . the next point.
2 I understand how . . . ., Christine but …
3 . . . ., but that is a management problem.
4 I'm . . . . I . . . . disagree on that one.
5 What exactly do . . . . by changes to work schedules?
6 . . . . that includes night shifts?

9 Susan McCarthy from Premier Dairies sent this email to her project team. Read it and decide whether the statements that follow are true (t) or false (f). Correct the false statements.

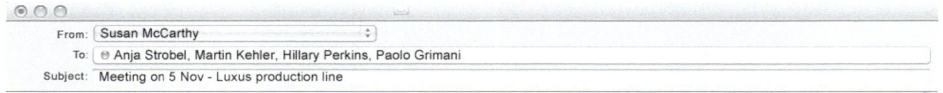

From: Susan McCarthy
To: Anja Strobel, Martin Kehler, Hillary Perkins, Paolo Grimani
Subject: Meeting on 5 Nov - Luxus production line

Dear colleagues,

I will have to postpone our meeting planned for 5th November on the subject of our new Luxus production line project. (I´ll inform you about a new date as soon as possible.) The reason is that the board has called another meeting for Thursday at 11 am, which I´ll have to attend.

There are two main points on the agenda. Firstly, the board wants to be informed about the staff's reaction to the new working hours (weekends, etc.) and secondly, they wish to discuss a possible change to the Luxus production line project. Management feels that the period for the testing phase should only be for three months instead of six. The board believes this will be good for us as we will be able to produce large quantities of the Luxus brand sooner. It is known that our competitors are behind us in the development of their own luxury dairy brands.

Could you please inform me by email if you think such a change to the timeline is possible? Please give me your ideas by tomorrow morning. I can then present them to the board at the meeting on Thursday.

Best regards,
Susan

1 Susan brought the Luxus production line meeting forward to 5th November.
2 There is a meeting planned with the board for Thursday at 11 am.
3 The board wants to know how the staff feel about the new working hours.
4 Management is thinking about increasing the testing phase to six months.
5 Premier Dairies' competitors are not developing their own luxury dairy brands.
6 Susan's colleagues should tell her what they think about the board's plans.

10 Match the words from the box to the words below. Then use these words to complete the sentences.

> high-end • market • premium • machine • contact • back-up

.... product	.... operators
.... pressure	.... details
.... price	.... plan

1 This new smartphone is a .... so we can sell it at a relatively high price.
2 There's so much .... we're going to have to reduce the price.
3 As this yogurt is a luxury brand we can put a .... on it: customers will still buy it.
4 Our .... make sure that all technical equipment runs smoothly on the production line.
5 I'll call her and make sure she gets the delivery. Can you give me her .... ?
6 Do you have a .... if the workers don't accept these conditions? We'll need an alternative.

11 Jane Smith, a new trainee at the company Foto-for-You, took a call yesterday. Listen to the phone call and correct her notes. She has made eight mistakes.

Caller: Jack Karouac
Company: Phonefine
Order: 57 calendars
Product number: EA837JH
Order: five camera stands
Product number: GH910DU
Delivery date: August 13th

Tip Wenn man im Englischen Begriffe buchstabiert, verwendet man das ICAO-Alphabet (*International Civil Aviation Organization*). Man sagt also beispielsweise 'b as in Bravo' oder 'b for Bravo' (siehe Kursbuch S. 53).

12 Read the sentences below and add the missing words to the puzzle. What is the word in column A?

1 We need to … the goods from China to Europe. The transport will take weeks.
2 Please send your … to this billing address.
3 Our basic price for each TV is €550, this includes a €50 … for transport.
4 "What's your … about the market?" "I think the situation will improve."
5 Payment is … by the end of the month. We must have the money then.
6 This is our … project. We're working on it now.
7 There are six stages in this project … . The project will take one year to complete.
8 Our … is to build a new factory in China because of the business opportunities there.
9 Deadlines are not fixed yet so they can change. They are not set in … .

13 You are giving a presentation on the latest business development. How would you express the following statements?

1 Prices will . . . . next year.   *stabil bleiben*
2 We believe that the number of orders will . . . .   *drastisch sinken*
 . . . .
3 As you can see from the chart, sales . . . .   *erreichten ihren Höhepunkt*
 . . . . in September.
4 . . . . regarding your question on   *Ich werde Ihnen Bescheid sagen*
 our sales in Eastern Europe.
5 The project will . . . . end   *bis … abgeschlossen sein*
 of May.

It's a deal 5

1 Have a look at the two conversations below. Choose the correct verb form to complete the sentences (simple present or *will* future).

Unit checklist
- discussing terms and negotiating a deal
- talking about differences
- comparing prices and terms

A: Will you be at the meeting tomorrow?

B: I don't know yet. I might attend if I will have/have[1] time, but it depends on my other appointments. I will let/let[2] you know later today.

A: By the way, what do you think of our supplier's new price for computer screens?

B: In my opinion, it's too high. If they won't reduce/don't reduce[3] it, we will have to cancel the contract. I'll call/call[4] them tomorrow to arrange a meeting to discuss it.

C: I'll agree to these new terms of delivery if you'll offer/offer[5] a guarantee of one year on the new machines.

D: That won't be easy. Our terms are already very good.

C: How about if we will increase/increase[6] our order?

D: I'll speak/speak[7] to my boss. Maybe we can offer a discount.

C: Great. Could you let me know what she says by next Monday?

2 Athlete Sports sells fitness equipment and has sent a sales letter and a catalogue to Lisa Smith. Read the letter and decide whether the statements that follow are true (t) or false (f). Correct the false statements.

Athlete Sports
20a Baysweather Road
London NW1 4LG
England

Lisa Smith
Scopicon Enterprises
Osborne Road
Birmingham B16 9JB
England

01.02.2012

Dear Lisa,

Customer satisfaction is very important to us at Athlete Sports. Our great team of sales experts will be happy to help you choose and purchase the right sports equipment for your needs. All Athlete Sports sales reps are qualified sports trainers so they can give you all the information you need to make the right decision. We also understand how important it is to provide good service before and after you buy a product. Have a look at our new catalogue to find out what we can offer you on our wide range of equipment from bicycles to weights machines.

As a special introductory offer, we would like to give all new customers a special discount of 15% on orders of at least €3,000 (£2,600). Hurry! This offer ends on 28 February.

The best thing about this deal is that we will take care of delivery and installation of the equipment in your home or office anywhere in Europe – free of charge! So, why don't you visit us at one of our shops to try the equipment? Check out our website www.athlete-sports.com to find your nearest shop.

We hope you will find our catalogue interesting and look forward to meeting you face to face at one of our many Athlete Sports branches around the country.

Kind regards,
Bill McLaren
(Sales director)

1. Athlete Sports employs qualified sports trainers as sales staff.
2. Athlete Sports' product range includes bicycles.
3. There is a special discount for orders of €3,000 and above.
4. The new special offer is available for eight weeks.
5. There is a separate charge for delivery.
6. Athlete Sports only sells its products online.

3 Sigrid Petik from Scopicon has a second meeting with Manfred Schmidt from Athlete Sports to discuss her previous order. Listen to their conversation and complete the sentences. Then listen again to check your answers.

1 Sigrid is really surprised because ....

2 About six weeks ago, Scopicon ....

3 Sigrid can increase the number of fitness machines because ....

4 Manfred offers free delivery for ....

Did you know?

Wenn um den Preis gefeilscht wird, spricht man im Englischen von 'to haggle'. Man kann diesen Ausdruck zwar auch in Geschäftskontexten verwenden, allerdings hat er dann oft einen negativen Unterton.

4 Do you remember what Sigrid and Manfred said at their meeting? Complete these sentences, then listen again to check.

1 Well, I'll tell .... I can give you a new discount of 10%.

2 Oh, ... Manfred. You can give us 15%, I'm sure.

3 If you increase the number of items, I .... to give you a bigger discount.

4 .... if we increase the number to twenty?

5 Yes, that's right. How does that ....?

6 That sounds ....

 Tip Wenn man einen Vorschlag macht (z. B. "Wie wär's mit …?") verwendet man im Englischen 'How about …?' oder 'What about …?'.

5 Complete the sentences with the correct comparative form of the adjectives.

1 I have an .... version of the photo software on my computer than you. (old)
2 Sales last year were .... than this year. (bad)
3 Our marketing department should be .... when passing on information to the public. (careful)

6 Read this article about Athlete Sports' market position. Choose the correct adjective for each gap.

> busier • larger • as strong as • highest • more expensive • less • most successful

As one of the ....¹ sports equipment producers in the world, Athlete Sports has a market share of around 20% in Europe which is ....² than many of its competitors. Athlete Sports is ....³ now than last year due to a sharp increase in demand. However, the future could be difficult because people could have ....⁴ money to spend as the economic crisis continues. The company may also have to increase the price of its products, which will probably make them ....⁵ than those of the competition. Quality control is also an issue. It must be of the ....⁶ standard so that Athlete Sports' future position in the market will be ....⁷ it is now.

7 Paul and Lorraine are talking about work-life balance. Listen and decide whether the statements below are true (t) or false (f). Correct the false statements.

1 ___ Lorraine used to work for a consultant.
2 ___ Lorraine's previous employer hired more staff because of the amount of work.
3 ___ Paul thinks the staff members should listen to each other.
4 ___ Paul used to work for a marketing company.
5 ___ There were extra payments for staff at Paul's previous company.

8 What do you do with your time outside work? Do you have a good work-life balance? What would you like to change? Write three to four sentences. *Over to you*

....

....

....

....

9 A visitor is speaking to a salesperson at a trade fair. Complete their conversation with the correct words from the box.

advance • delivery • depends • ex-works • include • offer • terms

A: So, can we talk about your general conditions? Can you give me some information?

B: Of course. What would you like to know?

A: Do your prices . . . . .¹ delivery and taxes?

B: No, that's extra, I'm afraid. All prices are . . . . .². And you'd have to pay for transport.

A: Oh, OK. What are your . . . . .³ of payment?

B: Normally, we ask for payment in . . . . .⁴, but in some cases we can arrange cash on . . . . .⁵.

A: I see. Do you . . . . .⁶ any discounts?

B: That really . . . . .⁷ on the size of the order ...

A: OK, thanks. I may come back with an order soon.

B: That would be great – but please take some brochures with you.

10 Match the words from the box to the words below. Then use these words to complete the sentences.

> bulk • bank • transport • company • order • account

....	discount	....	transfer
....	form	....	number
....	policy	....	costs

1 We can give a .... of 10% on large orders of over 3,000 pieces.
2 If you wish to purchase our fitness machines, please fill out this ....
3 Our .... is not to give discounts. Our board decided on this last month.
4 You can pay for the machines by cash, credit card or ....
5 If you let me know your .... at the Sparkasse Essen, I'll make sure you get the money by the beginning of next week.
6 For this delivery, we will pay for the .... from London to Edinburgh.

11 How would you translate the following comparisons? Use the words from the box.

> do sport • turnover (x2) • market • department • negotiations

1 Wir sind die kleinste Abteilung in der Firma, haben aber den meisten Umsatz.
2 Sie machen weniger Umsatz als wir.
3 Wir sind eine der erfolgreichsten Firmen in diesem Markt.
4 Die Verhandlungen waren nicht so schwierig wie wir dachten.
5 Arbeitnehmer die Sport treiben haben weniger Stress und finden es einfacher, sich zu konzentrieren.

Changing times   6

1 Form questions to fit the situation in each picture.

Unit checklist
- talking about experiences
- discussing and making arrangements
- updating a diary
- writing emails to make and change appointments

"............ ever ....?"
"Yes, I have. After the conference in Milan last year, I was stuck in traffic on the way to the airport and missed my flight. Luckily, I managed to get on another plane later that day."

"............ ever .... a meeting in a super-modern conference room?"
"Oh, you mean like the one on the top floor? No, but we're going to have a meeting up there next week."

"............ ever ....?"
"Yes, I went on a business trip to Birmingham last year. And I think I will go there more often next year as we are planning to set up a new office there."

"................................. the new photocopier yet? I need to copy these handouts for our meeting with marketing later today."
"No, sorry, I haven't. Let's go and ask Uta, she knows how to use the new machine."

Now answer the questions above so that they are true for you.

....
....
....
....

2 A radio journalist is interviewing Aysun Greenfield, who works for DPN. Listen to the interview. Are these statements true (t) or false (f)? Correct the false statements.

1 ___ Aysun has been at DPN for three months.
2 ___ Aysun has established a programme to help women working at DPN.
3 ___ Aysun and her colleagues have spoken to female students at university.
4 ___ Female employees at DPN are informed about additional qualifications.
5 ___ New female employees find the new programme helpful.
6 ___ Aysun wanted to study medicine.
7 ___ A teacher she knew at school advised her to study medicine.

3 Unscramble these sentences that are similar to what you heard in the interview in exercise 2.

1 been / I've / at / eight months. / about / the company / for / Well, actually

   ....

2 a programme / You've / at DPN. / established / also

   ....

3 to achieve / this? / you / are / What / doing

   ....

4 been / There / a lot / has / of / interest.

   ....

> **Tip** Wenn man auf höfliche Art und Weise eine gegenteilige Meinung ausdrücken möchte, kann man beispielsweise 'Well, actually …' verwenden, um die Aussage etwas abzuschwächen.

4 Read the text below and complete the sentences with the correct form of the verb (present perfect).

Hello everyone. I ....¹ (choose) this opportunity to introduce our new marketing manager to you. As you know, we held several interviews for this position. The successful candidate, Diana Webb, ...² (come) to us from a leading PR company based in Johannesburg, South Africa. She ....³ (lead) a number of innovative marketing campaigns and ....⁴ (develop) an impressive portfolio of clients. Naturally, we are very excited to see what changes she will make around here. I spoke to Diana this morning and she ....⁵ (agree) to give a short presentation at tomorrow's meeting to discuss some of her new ideas ...

5 Complete these sentences with the correct form of the verbs from the box (present perfect or simple past).

go (x2) • join • not stay • not apply • read

1 When ..... you ...... your company?
2 "......... you ever ...... to New York?" "No, but I'd like to go."
3 "Where's Wiebke?" "I think she .... out for some fresh air. She'll be back soon."
4 .... you .... our new brochure yet?
5 I .... in that hotel so far, but it looks nice.
6 He .... for a job last year because he was still at university.

6 What is the most interesting place you have been to? Was it on holiday or was it on a business trip? Name four things that make the place special.

over to you

....
....
....
....

7 David calls a colleague about arranging a meeting with a supplier. Listen and answer these questions.

1 Why does David want to bring the meeting forward?
2 Why can't Lana take part in the meeting at 10 am?
3 How will David reach his target price reduction of 5%?
4 Who is going to write the agenda?

> **Did you know?**
>
> Voraussetzung für jedes erfolgreiche Meeting sind eine Tagesordnung *(agenda)*, ggf. Unterlagen für die Teilnehmer *(handouts)* und ein Protokoll *(minutes)*. Fassen Sie am Ende zusammen, welche Punkte geklärt oder noch offen sind und wer welche Aufgaben bis wann übernimmt.

8 Complete these sentences with the correct form of the verbs (simple present or present continuous).

1 What time .... the flight .... (leave) tomorrow morning?
2 We .... (meet) our R&D manager tomorrow.
3 I .... (pick up) a customer from the airport tomorrow afternoon.
4 When .... the train .... (arrive) in London tomorrow?
5 What .... you .... (do) at 5 pm tomorrow?

9 Two colleagues are making an appointment. Read what they say and put the dialogue in a logical order.

Person A

1. I was wondering if we could make an appointment to discuss our new marketing campaign? Would tomorrow morning at 10 am suit you?
_ Fine. See you later.
_ OK, but shall we pencil it in anyway? Maybe you could tell me later today what your boss wants to do?
_ That's a shame. Well … how about 12 o'clock on Wednesday?

Person B

_ Yes, that would suit me. But my boss may want to see me on Wednesday and I can't say when exactly.
2. Let me see … no, unfortunately that time is inconvenient.
_ Yes, bye.
_ Yes, that should work out. I'll be able to confirm our appointment after I have spoken to him.

10 Read this text taken from the website of the Fyne Hotel in London.

The Fyne Hotel is the perfect location for meetings, conferences and seminars in the heart of London. All our seminar rooms have the most modern equipment, and you can be sure to receive the highest standard of service during your stay. We have a number of different seminar rooms big enough for 10 to 100 people. Please contact Kathy Wallace to find out more about our rooms and prices.

kathy.wallace@fyne-hotel.co.uk

You would like to hold a seminar at this hotel. Write an email to Kathy Wallace and include this information:

- you wish to hold a seminar on presentations from Monday, 04.08. to Wednesday, 06.08. for ten people
- find out if a room is available
- find out how much the hotel charges
- the Fyne Hotel should answer your email asap
- arrangements for this seminar must be finalized soon

11 Which words go together? Complete the sentences below by adding the most suitable word from the box.

> voicemail • meeting • follow-up • projector • plant

1 A colleague explained our new company structure, but we still had some

    . . . . questions.

2 We could discuss the contract at a breakfast . . . . tomorrow morning. I'll organize some coffee.

3 I got your . . . . message this morning. I'm afraid I was in a meeting so my mobile was off.

4 He's our . . . . manager. He is responsible for the whole factory.

5 I can show you my presentation, but I need a data . . . . Is there one available?

12 Read the sentences below and add the missing words to the puzzle. What is the word in column A?

1. CeBIT is an international trade … for the digital industry which is held in Hanover.
2. We must … our customers with good arguments about our new product. They will then choose us as their supplier.
3. I'm afraid I have to cancel the meeting. I'm really sorry for the … .
4. She is able to do many different jobs and tasks. She really is very … .
5. The verb form of the adjective 'valuable' is to … .
6. I'm calling to… the appointment you suggested. I can attend the meeting tomorrow at 11.30.
7. I'm so sorry but your goods are going to be late. I have to … for this.
8. The verb form of the adjective 'successful' is to … .

		A							
		1 F							
	2 C			N					
	3 I				I				
4 A		P							
	5 V								
	6 C								
7 A		G							
	8 S			E					

13 Read the sentences below. Which is correct – a or b?

1. Unser Flug geht um 8.00 Uhr morgen früh.
   a We leave tomorrow at 8 am.
   b Our flight leaves at 8 am tomorrow.
2. Wie lange kennen Sie John schon?
   a How long have you known John?
   b How long did you know John?
3. Haben Sie den Lieferanten schon angerufen?
   a Have you phoned the supplier yet?
   b Did you phone the supplier yet?
4. Bitte schreiben Sie den Bericht bis Montag fertig.
   a Please finish the report before Monday.
   b Please finish the report by Monday.

Progress check 2 → page 67

Out of the office 7

1 Today is Wednesday and Lisa has already completed a couple of tasks this week. Have a look at her diary. What else has or hasn't she done this week?

Unit checklist
- talking about recent activities and new developments
- practising small talk and saying goodbye
- making polite complaints
- listening for information in presentations

	Mo 21 May	Tue 22 May	Wed 23 May	Thu 24 May	Fri 25 May
9.00					
10.00	compile sales figures		check travel options	finish agenda	confirm travel arrangements
11.00		prepare agenda			
12.00					
1.00		take minutes – R&D meeting			
2.00					
3.00		present sales figures to board			
4.00					
5.00				send minutes to team	

1. Lisa took the minutes at the R&D meeting on Tuesday, but she . . . . the minutes to everyone in the team yet.
2. She compiled the sales figures on Monday morning. Since then she . . . . the sales figures to the board.
3. She started preparing the agenda earlier this week but . . . . it yet.
4. She checked travel options for her boss but still . . . . the travel arrangements yet.

2 Two members of staff are talking about a new brochure. Complete the dialogue with the correct form of the verbs in brackets (present perfect) and with either *for* or *since*.

Peter: Cathy, we .haven't talked..... ¹ (not talk) about our new brochure ....² (for/since) some time so can you give me a quick overview of the present situation?

Cathy: Sure. Over the last month, we .... ³ (spend) quite a lot of time looking at different ideas. In fact, I .... just .... ⁴ (have) a look at the new photographs. Some of them are quite good.

Peter: So I see....................... ⁵ (you, decide) which ones to use?

Cathy: No I haven't actually, because I still .... ⁶ (not receive) all the texts for the brochure yet.

Peter: Oh yes – sorry Cathy. I forgot to give them to you. They .... ⁷ (be) on my desk .... ⁸ (for/since) last Monday. I'll make sure you get them.

3 John and Sarah are talking about their company and their plans for the future.
🔊 16 Listen to their conversation and answer these questions.

1 How much has the turnover increased by?
2 Why does the company need capital?
3 How much is paid every month for the company's loan?
4 What is the interest rate for mortgages?
5 Why doesn't Sarah like the idea of getting new partners?
6 Why should Sarah and John speak to the banks together?

> **Did you know?**
>
> *IPO* steht für 'initial public offering' (Aktienerstemission). Indem Anleger Aktien kaufen, erhöht eine Gesellschaft beim ersten Börsengang ihr Kapital für geplante Investitionen.

4 A journalist is interviewing a businessman. Complete the sentences below with the correct form of the words in the box (simple past or present perfect).

> discuss • do • establish • go • have • increase • not make • speak

A: So, how well is your company doing in the market?

B: Well, as you know, we ....¹ it four years ago in New York, and since then our turnover ....² sharply. Demand for our machines is growing so we need capital to expand.

A: I see........ you ....³ to any bank managers yet?

B: I ....⁴ meetings with three so far. Their conditions for loans are all interesting, but we ....⁵ any final decision yet.

A: Choosing can't be easy.

B: Well, I ....⁶ our plans with a bank in Chicago last week. The meeting ....⁷ quite well. Their terms are slightly better than those of other banks, and they ....⁸ a lot of business recently with companies like ours so we'll probably decide on them.

5 Read the interview in exercise 4 again. Highlight the words that signal the simple past or the present perfect.

6 Two business people say goodbye to each other. Read what they say and put the dialogue in a logical order.

Person A

1 Well, that was a good meeting.

  That's fine. So … have a good trip home and keep in touch.

  Would you like me to call you a taxi?

  Thank you. Bye.

  Well, it's been good seeing you again. Give my regards to Sonja when you see her next.

Person B

  Sure, I'll tell her you said hello. And thanks again for lunch.

  Yes, it was. I'm afraid I'll have to go now though – my flight leaves in two hours.

  No, thanks. I think I'll take the underground.

  I will, Tessa. Thanks a lot. Bye.

7 **What is the best hotel you have ever stayed in? Why did you like it? What were the four most important features?** *over to you*

....
....
....
....

8 **Last week, Mike O'Sullivan took a client out for lunch. Unfortunately, he was not pleased with the service. Have a look at the two situations below, and complete the dialogues with the words from the box.**

> I'm sorry to say that • actually • I'm very sorry • Let me take

Mike: Excuse me! Excuse me …!

Waiter: Yes, sir. Is everything OK?

Mike: Well, ...¹ no. ....² there's minced meat in my Lasagna. I ordered the vegetarian Lasagna because I really don't like minced meat.

Waiter: ....³, sir. ....⁴ this back to the kitchen. I'll bring the right dish straight away.

> I'm really sorry • Unfortunately • How about • I'm afraid

Mike: ....⁵ that the food wasn't great tonight. ....⁶ the other restaurant was fully booked.

Client: Oh, don't worry about it. It wasn't too bad. Once they brought the vegetarian Lasagna it was fine.

Mike: I know a nice French café just around the corner. ....⁷ if we go there for coffee?

Client: ....⁸ I'm a bit short on time. I'm really sorry, but maybe we could go there next time?

9 Complete the sentences below with words from the box. Be careful: there are two words you do not need.

> any (2x) • anyone • anything • anywhere • some • someone • something • somewhere

1 Could I speak to .... about your product range, please?
2 Do you have .... information about our sales for this year?
3 I don't know .... about our turnover for last month.
4 There isn't .... to sit.
5 I'm sorry, but there aren't .... rooms available at the moment.
6 .... is wrong with our order. We'll have to contact the supplier.
7 Would you like .... coffee?

10 Sue Jones is giving a presentation about her company's sales performance in the United States and Europe. Listen and answer these questions.

1 How did Sue's company make a successful start in the US?
2 Sue's company is not meeting its sales targets in the US. What are the two main reasons?
3 Why have sales risen by 15% in Europe?
4 She thinks more money should be invested in advertising. Why does she think so?

11 Do you remember what Sue said? Complete these sentences, then listen again to check.

1 As Tom mentioned, ... you about our recent sales performance.
2 My presentation .... twenty minutes.
3 If you don't ...., I'd like to take questions ....
4 I'd like to .... this slide which shows our falling sales figures in the US.
5 So, ... on to our business situation in Europe.
6 So, ... our business opportunities for the future?

Tip Wenn Sie eine Präsentation geben, führen Sie auf Ihren Folien nur die wichtigsten Informationen in Stichworten auf. Denken Sie daran, dass Sie für die Präsentation vor Publikum etwa ein Drittel länger brauchen, als beim Üben. Als Grundsatz gilt dabei das Prinzip KISS – *keep it short and simple*.

12 Read the sentences below and add the missing words to the puzzle. What is the word in column A?

1. There will be around 20 … taking part in the meeting.
2. A loan from a bank to buy a house is called a ….
3. Tell me, what are the pros and … of the project?
4. The … of this meeting is to develop ideas for new products.
5. We had a … meeting at the beginning of the project.
6. I've got a loan from the bank with an … rate of 3.5%.
7. My bank has … in many cities around the country.
8. I'm going to speak to my colleagues in Moscow in a … meeting. I won't physically meet them.

```
                             A
     1 P │ │ │ │ C │ │ │ │ │
                 2 M │ │ │ A │ │
                     3 C │ │ │ │
                 4 P │ │ │ O │
             5 k │ │ │ - │
         6 l │ │ │ │
             7 B │ │ │ C │ │ │
         8 v │ │ │ │
```

13 Read the sentences below and complete the translations.

1. Wie lange haben Sie Ihr Büro schon?

   How long ....?

2. Darf ich Ihnen den Mantel abnehmen?

   Let me ....

3. Bitte richten Sie Sarah viele Grüße von mir aus.

   .... to Sarah.

4. Könnte ich bitte ein Glas Wein haben?

   Could I ...., please?

5. Zögern Sie nicht, Fragen zu stellen.

   Feel ....

At a trade fair

Unit checklist
- describing features and benefits of products
- distinguishing formal and informal emails
- reading a report

1 Complete this memo about arrangements for a trade fair. Choose the correct words from the box.

benefits • forthcoming • retailers • display stands • substantial • warehouse • giveaways

As we're planning to take part in the ....¹ trade fair in London next year, I would like to update you on how arrangements are going. I've contacted a company that can provide us with some ....² so that we can show our products to visitors. They say they still have some available in their ....
..................³, so delivery shouldn't be a problem. I am also organizing some
..................⁴ for visitors – free pens, calendars etc. The ....
..................⁵ are clear; people always like to have something for free and there is a good chance that visitors will remember our company name.
I am convinced that a lot of ....⁶ will attend this trade fair. They all have shops in city centres around the country and sell to the end customer. I am certain that they will place a ....⁷ number of orders after the fair because demand for our products has risen sharply over the last year.

2 Uli phones his colleague to talk about the UK market. Listen to their conversation and complete these sentences with the correct information.

1 Another UK retailer has placed a .... order for five ....
2 The marketing department of this UK retailer plans a campaign focussing on
 ....
3 The UK retailer thinks customers are willing to pay slightly more for ....
 ....
4 The colour of the product sometimes changes because of ....
5 A sales team should be .... for the UK market.
6 At the moment, the German office could deal with ....
7 If people are hired too early, it may be ....

3 Uli puts together some information about future business opportunities. Complete this extract with the correct expression from the box.

> Although • As a result • because • due to • however • such as • In addition

The latest sales figures show our recent success in countries ....¹ the UK and Ireland and indicate that we will be able to increase turnover there in the future. We do, ...², need to be careful about expanding our market area – especially ....³ our disappointing performance in Central Europe. ....⁴ of this poor performance, it is clear that we need to make some changes.

I suggest that we reduce our operations in Central Europe and focus on expanding our successful markets instead. ....⁵, I propose that we establish a sales team in Manchester ....⁶ UK orders currently have to be dealt with in Germany. ....⁷ this would initially increase our costs, we would soon see the benefits of being closer to our clients.

> **Did you know?**
>
> Der Begriff ‚Außendienst' kann mit 'sales force' oder 'field sales force' übersetzt werden. Das Wort 'field' betont die Tatsache, dass der/die Außendienstmitarbeiter/in für einen bestimmten geografischen Bereich zuständig ist.

4 Match the words from the two boxes to complete the sentences below.

1	badly	a	interesting
2	clearly	b	designed
3	highly	c	seen
4	warmly	d	welcomed

1 The delivered parts were not of the quality we wanted. They were ....

2 The benefits of the trade fair could be .... by everyone.

3 We found their latest offer .... We'll certainly place an order with them.

4 They were .... by the Chinese delegation in Beijing. They were also invited for lunch.

48 Unit **8** At a trade fair

5 Rewrite these sentences as in the example. Use an adjective and the infinitive.

1. Solving the problem was quite difficult.
   It was quite difficult to solve the problem.
2. Responding to her request wasn't easy.
   ....
3. Dealing with that customer has been almost impossible.
   ....
4. Operating our new machines was simple.
   ....

6 Complete the sentences with the correct form of the verbs in brackets (past perfect).

1. Until last week, I .... (not take) a sick day in over two years.
2. When I got to my office, the supplier ...... already .... (call) twice.
3. He didn't notice the spelling mistakes in his CV until after he .... (send) his job application.
4. ...... the meeting already .... (start) when you arrived?

7 Select the correct verb form to complete the text: simple past or past perfect?

During our presentation last week, we outlined / had outlined¹ the benefits of our products to the customer and then we told / had told² them about our prices. They gave / had given³ us an idea of their budget beforehand, so we knew / had known⁴ our prices were OK for them. After the presentation, they invited / had invited⁵ us to join them for lunch. While we were walking there, they asked / had asked⁶ me if I had brought / brought⁷ some product samples with me, but unfortunately I didn't think / hadn't thought⁸ of bringing some along. I promised / had promised⁹ to send them as soon as I get back. When I returned / had returned¹⁰ the next day, I found / had found¹¹ out that our secretary sent / had sent¹² some samples the day before.

8 Read this informal email sent from Steven Capaldi to Paula Docherty. Match sentences 1-8 with an equivalent formal sentence (a-h).

Hi Paula,

I'll be in your neck of the woods in Berlin next week on Tuesday, Oct 11 visiting some suppliers so can we touch base at your company?**1** I want to discuss any future orders we may make.**2** How about meeting at 11 o'clock on Tuesday?**3** Just send me a quick email if this time is OK for you.**4** BTW, a colleague of mine also told me you have a new brochure.**5** Can you send me a copy by Monday?**6** There might be some new and interesting products we could talk about at our meeting on Tuesday.**7**

Hope to hear from you soon!**8**

Best wishes,
Steven

a That way, we could talk about any changes to your product range at our meeting on Tuesday.
b Could you please confirm whether this time is convenient for you?
c Would 11 o'clock suit you for a meeting?
d I would appreciate it if you could send me a copy by Monday of next week.
e I'm going to visit some suppliers in Berlin next week on Tuesday, October 11th, and I was wondering if you have time for a quick meeting.
f By the way, a colleague of mine mentioned that a new catalogue is available.
g I would like to discuss any future orders we may place with TSE.
h I look forward to hearing from you.

9 Listen to this podcast about an electric car. Then answer the questions below.

1 What is the problem with the back of the car?
2 How much does the car cost?
3 Why is the car useful for people who drive a lot in cities?
4 How can customer awareness be improved?
5 What is the main drawback that Bill mentions?
6 Why do European manufacturers have to be quicker than their Asian competitors?

50 Unit **8** At a trade fair

10 A member of a sales team has written the report below. Read it and decide whether the statements that follow are true (t) or false (f). Correct the false statements.

Terms of reference
Our CEO, Juan de Cusa, requested this report about the proposal made at the last sales and marketing meeting at our headquarters in Berlin on 01.10. to lease five electric cars for our sales team in Madrid.

Aims
The aims of this report are to compare the benefits and drawbacks of such a plan and to give a recommendation to management.

Findings
At a separate meeting held at our Spanish office on 10.10., I was informed about how much the sales team travels. They have a large number of customers and work on a tight schedule so they need to be flexible. Furthermore there were some concerns about distances, as some sales reps are required to drive up to 80 kilometres per day. They currently have to use their own cars for this – our company compensates them, but the staff thought the amount was not enough. On average, we compensate each sales rep with €200 per month. Before we met the team, we had already found out that the cost of leasing five electric cars could be up to €2,500 per month. In my opinion, this is the only real drawback of the proposal.

Speculation
The sales team supports the leasing of five cars as they could use them to visit customers around the region without having to use their own cars. I see two possible benefits: the leasing project could be good for the morale of the sales team, and we could use the cars to advertise the company name (for example with a logo on each car). Despite the fact that the cost of leasing is higher than the travelling costs the sales reps currently have, these two advantages should not be ignored by management.

Conclusion and recommendation
Based on these arguments, I feel that we should go ahead with this plan, and I recommend that management give its approval. I could make sure that the cars are delivered by the end of next month.

---

1 ____ The sales team in Madrid requested the report.
2 ____ A meeting was held at the Spanish offices on October 10th.
3 ____ Sales reps in Madrid currently use their own cars to visit customers.
4 ____ On average, the sales reps get €2,500 compensation per month.
5 ____ The only drawback of the proposal is the cost issue.
6 ____ Team morale is a factor that should be considered by management.
7 ____ The electric cars could be used for advertising.
8 ____ The recommendation is not to lease the electric cars.

Tip Berichte werden je nach Inhalt, Funktion und Adressaten unterschieden. Ein *situational* oder *informational report* präsentiert einen Status bzw. eine Ausgangslage. Ein *analytical report* legt darüber hinaus meist auch Empfehlungen zu einer Entscheidung dar. In allen Formen ist die Struktur dabei ähnlich *(terms of reference, aims, findings* usw.).

11 Describe a product or service that your company sells. What are the top two benefits to the customer? *over to you*

....
....
....

12 Which words go together? Complete the sentences below by adding the most suitable word from the box.

> sales • panels • features • electric • ratings

1 Please let me have your report on the new solar .... by Monday.
2 The .... car was our best-selling product last month.
3 The car's extra .... were presented at the trade fair.
4 Because of poor .... performance, one of the car models will have to be discontinued.
5 The report compares customer .... from this year and last year and makes some recommendations.

13 Read the sentences below and complete the translations.

1 Wir haben sichergestellt, dass unsere Anweisungen leicht zu verstehen sind.
   .... our instructions are easy to understand.
2 Ich wäre Ihnen sehr dankbar, wenn Sie die Broschüren bis spätestens Montag schicken könnten.
   .... if you could send the brochures by Monday at the latest.
3 Der Preis ist eigentlich ziemlich günstig kalkuliert, wenn man alle Vorteile berücksichtigt.
   It's .... priced if you consider all the benefits.
4 Obwohl es nicht so viele Besucher auf der Messe gab, wie wir erhofft hatten, war unser Stand gut besucht.
   .... there weren't .... to the fair as we had hoped, our stand was well attended.

52 Unit **8** At a trade fair

Culture matters 9

Unit checklist
- talking about a company's history
- making conversation at a restaurant
- making and dealing with complaints

1 Frank and Allan meet in the canteen at work. Complete their conversation with the correct words from the box.

> be fine • at a seminar • compared to • for a few days • settled into • looking forward to • What kind of

Frank: Hi Allan. I haven't seen you .... ¹.

Allan: Yes, I've been away. I was .... ². Did I tell you that I'm going on a new international assignment soon?

Frank: No, I don't think you did. .... ³ assignment is it?

Allan: I'm going to be based in Romania to help set up our new production plant in Bucharest.

Frank: Wow, that sounds really interesting.

Allan: Yes, I'm really .... ⁴ it. I'm excited about getting to know the local culture and adapting to a new working environment. But leaving my friends and colleagues behind certainly won't be easy. Then once I've .... ⁵ everything, I'd like my family to join me in Romania.

Frank: Yes, I see what you mean. But I'm sure you'll .... ⁶.

Allan: I hope so. It'll certainly be more challenging .... ⁷ other jobs I've done in the past.

2 Listen to the conversation between three HR managers, and answer these questions.

1. What will happen to the employees in Glasgow?
2. How is Romania supporting the company?
3. What will the staff from Glasgow do in Bucharest?
4. Who has been preparing for the project for about a week?
5. What has Paula been thinking about for quite some time?
6. Who should Dave get in touch with?

3 **What did Paula and Richard form exercise 2 say? Complete these sentences, then listen again to check.**

1 Well, that brings us to the next point on the agenda – ....
   .... from our plant in Glasgow to the new one in Bucharest.
2 The plant in Bucharest will save the company ....
3 During that period, our technical staff has been showing the new Romanian employees .... the machines.
4 The machines we will use in Romania are ....
   as the ones we have been using in Glasgow for the last two years.
5 The Romanian workers have been studying English since Romania started
   ....
6 It's just not that easy to find a company that provides ....
   .... for employees relocating to Romania.

> **Tip** Neben unterschiedlichen Löhnen (*salaries*) ist der Ausbau von Kapazitäten in anderen Ländern auch wegen staatlicher Subventionen (*subsidies*) und günstiger Körperschaftssteuern (*corporate* oder *company tax*) attraktiv.

4 **Read this email Cullen's CEO sent to his employees.**

From: Paula Fields
To: Office 1; Office 2; Office 3
Subject: Looking back and moving forward

Cullen Enterprises dates back to 1925 when Peter Cullen set up this company in Glasgow where it grew for more than 50 years. Since its foundation in 1925, the company has reinvented itself more than once. Founder Peter Cullen started off as young engineer here in Glasgow and developed mechanical devices that kicked off production of the first telephones. Since the 1950s, Cullen Enterprises has also been producing mechanical parts for cameras.

When Peter's son, John Cullen, took over back in 1975, he realized the challenges in the changing market, and we have been growing ever since.

The motto that describes our company best must therefore be: 'nothing is more constant than change'. I would like to thank you all for being so flexible, especially regarding the proposed transfer of some of our technical staff to Romania. We appreciate your cooperation.

Now decide whether the statements below are true (t) or false (f). Correct the false statements.

1   The CEO sent the email because Cullen Enterprises hasn't been developing over the last couple of months.
2   The company has always been successful with the same product.
3   Cullen Enterprises has been producing parts for telephones since its early days.
4   The company has always been based in Scotland.

5 Complete these sentences with the correct from of the verbs in brackets (present perfect simple or present prefect continuous).

Cullen is relocating, but not closing down

Over the past few years, Romania ....
.... ¹ (offer) financial support to companies relocating to their country. The low corporate tax in many Eastern European countries ....
.... ² (make) relocating production facilities even more attractive.

The Glasgow-based company Cullen Enterprises takes advantage of these factors. Company representative Andrew Neill said: "We .... ³ (discuss) these plans for more than a year, and it .... ⁴ (become clear) to us that moving part of our production to Romania will save jobs here in the UK. We ....
.... ⁵ (achieve) significant growth since 1990, and it would be wrong to ignore what our employees .... ⁶ (add) to our success."

6 Two American businessmen are eating at a restaurant in Munich. Complete this extract of their conversation with the correct words from the box.

> here's • kind • order • main • recommend • speciality • starter

A: So, what are you going to . . . . ¹?

B: To be honest, I don't really know.

A: Well, I can . . . . .² the Münchner Weißwurst.

B: Right, but what is it exactly?

A: It's a . . . . .³ of sausage, and it's a local . . . . .⁴. You should try it. It's nice.

B: OK, that sounds good. Well, ...⁵ to our new project.

A: Yes, cheers.

Waiter: Excuse me, are you ready to order now?

B: Yes, I'll have the asparagus soup as a . . . . .⁶, and I'd like the Münchner Weißwurst as my . . . . .⁷ course.

> **Did you know?**
>
> Wenn Sie im Ausland Trinkgeld *(tip)* geben, sollten Sie die dortigen Gepflogenheiten beachten. In den USA ist das Trinkgeld fester Bestandteil des Lohns der Servicekräfte (15-20%). In vielen asiatischen Ländern gilt es dagegen als unhöflich, Service mit Trinkgeld zu honorieren.

7 Unscramble these sentences.

1 to go for lunch / with the customer / She / expect me / didn't

. . . .

2 to order / some drinks / for you / Would you / like me

. . . . ?

3 me / not to eat / They warned / the local food

. . . .

4 I advise / during lunch / not / politics or religion / you / to talk about

. . . .

8 Listen to Sophie Dupont making a complaint. Are these statements true (t) or false (f)? Correct the false statements.

1. ___ The order number for the consignment is YO-213-ST.
2. ___ There were too few chairs in the consignment.
3. ___ James offers a discount of 5% on the current order.
4. ___ Sophie will send the damaged chairs back to James' company.

9 Do you remember what Sophie and James said? Complete these sentences, then listen to track 21 again to check.

1. Oh dear, I'm sorry ....
2. Well, obviously, something has .... here.
3. I'll .... straight away.
4. I .... again for the ....

10 James writes to Sophie about the delivery of the chairs. Select the correct words from the box to complete his email.

promise • apologize • avoid • dissatisfied • in touch • Regarding

Dear Ms Dupont,

I would like to . . ..¹ again for the broken chairs that you received yesterday. I have got ....² with our shipping department, and they have informed me that fifteen new chairs will be sent to you.

..............³ the damaged chairs, I have arranged for them to be collected tomorrow at twelve o'clock. I realize you must be quite ....⁴ with our service at the moment, but I can ....⁵ you that we will do everything we can to ....⁶ such problems in the future.

11 Have you ever had to complain about a service or product? Describe what happened. Write four sentences.

over to you

12 Which words go together? Complete the sentences below by adding the most suitable word from the box.

> code • career • prices • department • style • corporate • values

1 English is our company's . . . . language.
2 Our company . . . . include providing good customer care, building staff morale and respecting colleagues.
3 The board's management . . . . is quite open. All employees can speak to them directly.
4 The dress . . . . here is quite formal Mondays to Thursdays, but you can wear jeans on Fridays.
5 The shipping . . . . is responsible for moving goods around the world.
6 We offer competitive . . . . on all our products. On average, they are 5% below those of our competitors.
7 You should attend seminars if you want a higher position in the company. Further training is good for your . . . . advancement.

13 Read the sentences below. Which is correct – a or b?

1 Wir stellen bereits seit zehn Jahren Computerteile her.
   a   We've been producing computer equipment for more than ten years.
   b   We produced computer equipment for ten years.
2 Ich fühle mich seit ein paar Tagen nicht so gut.
   a   I didn't feel very well.
   b   I haven't been feeling very well for a few days.
3 Wie lange bieten sie schon interkulturelles Training an?
   a   How long have they been providing cross-cultural training?
   b   How long have they provided cross-cultural training?
4 Ich habe mir Ihr neuestes Angebot noch nicht durchgelesen.
   a   I haven't been reading your most recent offer yet.
   b   I haven't read your most recent offer yet.

Smooth operations

Unit checklist
- talking about supply chains
- discussing hypothetical situations and consequences
- talking about future training plans

1 Use the words from the flowchart to complete the supply chain process below. Then put the sentences in the correct order.

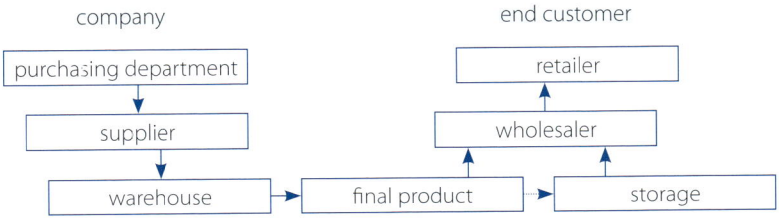

1 Whenever a customer orders a product, our .purchasing department. places an order for the necessary components with the supplier.

   Finally, the . . . . can purchase the final product from the retailer.

   Then, the supplier sends these components to our . . . .

   After that, the components are assembled in the production process to make the . . . .

   The wholesaler delivers this product to the . . . .

   It is then either put into . . . . or transported straight to the wholesaler.

2 A team of purchasers are having a meeting. Listen to what they say, and answer these questions.

1. When were the purchasing guidelines created?
2. What are the advantages to the company of having a single European strategy?
3. Why might Steffi and her team at headquarters still have to convince their colleagues in the company's subsidiaries?
4. How can they get the message across?
5. What should be published on the intranet?

Did you know?
Bei Verträgen wird ein Gerichtsstand *(jurisdiction)* vereinbart, damit verbindlich festgelegt ist, nach welchem (Landes)recht evtl. später auftretende Probleme verhandelt werden.

3 Do you remember what was said at the meeting in exercise 2? Complete these sentences, then listen again to check.

1 If we set up a single European strategy, it . . . . give us more advantages.
2 If we don't do that, we . . . . get anywhere.
3 If we . . . . that, there would be a good chance that we'd get the message across.
4 But what would we do if purchasers . . . . follow the guidelines even after all our proposals?

4 Match these sentence halves to make first or second conditional sentences.

1 I wouldn't do that
2 The supplier could give us a discount
3 We can meet again tomorrow to discuss the price
4 We won't supply the goods to them
5 What will you do
6 Would he accept delivery

a   if we paid him quickly.
b   if you like.
c   if his consignment arrived late?
d   if I were you.
e   if the customer complains?
f   if they don't pay in advance.

5 Complete these sentences with the correct form of the verbs in brackets (second conditional sentences).

1 If we .increased... (increase) our budget, we .wouldn't have. (not have) any problems with production schedules. Unfortunately, the budget is already tight.
2 They will probably say no, but if the board . . . . (approve) our plan at next week's meeting, we . . . . (can/improve) our distribution process.
3 If I . . . . (be) you, I . . . . (speak) to the boss about the problem before it gets any worse.
4 Unfortunately, there isn't much demand for the product, but if our turnover . . . . (rise), we . . . . (can/pay) our employees more.

5   Imagine a worst-case scenario: What .... (happen) if the supplier .... (go) out of business?
6   "What .... we .... (do) if they .... (cancel) the contract?" "Stop worrying! That won't happen."

6 **The head of a purchasing team has written a report. Read it and decide whether the statements that follow are true (t) or false (f). Correct the false statements.**

Summary
This report looks at problems in our supply chain due to the fact that our main tier-one supplier for storage devices in Spain has gone out of business. We will only be able to produce our tablet PCs for the next three weeks because we will run out of storage devices after this period. It is therefore essential to find another supplier as quickly as possible. If we do not find a new supplier soon, we may encounter a large number of difficulties in the future.

Findings
Four members of the purchasing department visited two companies – Sedlak in the Czech Republic and Kostov in Bulgaria – to find out whether one or both of these companies could provide us with storage devices in the near future and in the long term. Both companies offer these devices at the standard retail price. However, we found out during our meeting with Sedlak, that their order books are full for the next six months and there would be no opportunity for them to supply us at the moment. On the other hand, Kostov could provide us with what we need quickly but their quality standards are low. If we bought these components from Kostov, our company reputation could be badly damaged.

Conclusion
Finding another supplier will not be easy. However, because we need to move quickly, we could contact Kostov again to at least help us out in the immediate future. Quality would still be an issue, but we may be able to solve this if action is taken. In the long term, it would be better to work with Sedlak as this company is well-established in the European market and has done business with German customers in the past.

Recommendation
It is recommended to management that we place an order with Kostov, but we should send a team of experts to this company to assist them with quality management. However, it is also recommended that we build up our business relationship with Sedlak to make sure that we have a safe supply level in the long term.

1   There are enough storage devices in stock to produce tablet PCs for the next year.
2   Sedlak and Kostov sell their products below retail price.
3   Kostov cannot supply storage devices in the short term.
4   Sedlak sold storage devices to German companies in the past.

7 **Have a look at the statements and complete them so that they are true.**

1. We .... (run out) of storage devices within three weeks if we don't find another supplier soon.
2. If Sedlak had more capacities, they .... (can provide) more devices.
3. If we .... (want) to ensure safe supplies in the long term, we would have to build up our business relationship with Sedlak.
4. If Kostov .... (not have) quality issues, we wouldn't have to send a team of experts.

8 **The sentences below are budget talk. Add the missing words to the puzzle. What is the word in column A?**

1. Because of recent budget … we've had to reduce the amount of business trips we make.
2. Because management increased our budget, we're making good … in the project.
3. I'm not … for the budget. This is decided by our head of department.
4. We're … budget. We're spending too much money.
5. To get a budget increase you'll have to make a full … analysis.
6. If we received a budget increase, we would certainly double our return on … .
7. We'll have to increase our … budget for all the staff and materials we need for our department.

1. C
2. P
3. R
4. O
5. S · T
6. I
7. O P

9 **Complete these sentences with *unless* or *in case*.**

1. .... we increase our budget, we won't be able to update our IT systems.
2. We should also write the product description in French .... we have to deal with any French customers in the future.

3 I'll just take my laptop to the meeting .... people would like to see some pictures of our new offices.

4 I think the agenda for our meeting with the supplier is finished .... you have anything else to add.

5 We'll keep some extra components in stock .... there is a sudden increase in orders.

6 We won't increase our production levels .... there is more demand from the market.

10 James is having a staff appraisal meeting with his boss. Listen and answer the questions below.

1 What level of German has James reached?
2 What happens when he calls his colleagues in Austria?
3 What are the advantages of web-based training according to Lisa?
4 What issue is management discussing at the moment?
5 What would James like to do at London University?
6 How could the company help him with his plans?

> **Tip** Unter www.cornelsen.de/business-english finden Sie zusätzliche Arbeitsblätter und abwechslungsreiche Online-Übungen um Ihre Englischkenntnisse weiter auszubauen.

11 What is your goal for next year? Think about something you would like to achieve in business (e.g. learn a new language, expand your IT knowledge). How are you going to reach your goal?

Over to you

....
....
....
....

12 Have a look at the blue words. Which words go together? Match these sentence halves.

1. Our products are delivered to our shops through a distribution
2. We order a lot of standard
3. According to our sales
4. We operate under a tight
5. Our customer has made an unreasonable
6. Do we have a back-up

___ budget. There isn't much money left at the end of the year.
___ agent based in Leeds.
___ request. They want us to supply the smartphones by tomorrow. That's simply not possible.
___ components from our tier-one suppliers. The parts have not been customized.
___ plan if the supplier can't deliver the components? Can we get them from someone else?
___ statistics, our turnover has been increasing steadily over the last year.

13 Have a look at the dialogue below. Can you add the missing words?

A: Wenn wir unsere Lieferzeiten nicht verbessern, werden unsere Kunden ihre Bestellungen stornieren.
B: Was schlagen Sie vor?
A: Das Problem ist unser jetziger Lieferant. Wenn er die Fristen nicht einhalten kann, müssen wir uns nach jemand anderem umsehen.
B: Sie haben recht. Wir brauchen eine Lösung, um keine Kunden an die Konkurrenz zu verlieren.

A: If we . . . . our delivery times, our customers . . . .
. . . .
B: What would . . . .?
A: Our current . . . . causes all the problems. If he . . . .
. . . ., we . . . . somebody else.
B: You're right. We need a solution . . . . not to lose . . . . .
. . . .

✓ Progress check 3 → page 69

Progress check 1 — Unit 1-3

Check your English in units 1-3. Look at these questions (1-25) and tick the correct answer (only one is correct). You get one point for each correct solution.

Company organisation & responsibilities   Points

1. Our company has a number of different … in Europe.
   a subsidiaries   b works council   c parent companies
   d department
2. She … on a special project at the moment.
   a works   b is working   c work   d working
3. While I … in Asia, I met some suppliers in Beijing.
   a travel   b am travelling   c travelled   d was travelling
4. He works for the HR department. HR stands for … .
   a Human Resources   b High Research   c Human Risk
   d High Risk
5. She … her office late yesterday. There was a lot to do.
   a is leaving   b left   c leaves   d leave
6. I'm responsible … developing our product range.
   a for   b from   c in   d of

Personal information   Points

7. "What does she do?" "She's … sales."
   a at   b in   c for   d on
8. I … in Berlin, but I moved to Cologne last year.
   a live   b am   c was living   d used to live
9. I … finish my project yesterday.
   a can   b am able to   c was able to   d able
10. "When … your company?" "Oh, about five years ago."
    a do you join   b you join   c you joined   d did you join
11. "What … ?" "He's a call centre agent."
    a does he   b he does   c is he doing   d does he do
12. After … from the University of Augsburg in 1991 with a degree in mechanical engineering, Ruth joined our company to work in the R&D department.
    a graduating   b graduate   c graduates   d graduated

Socializing & exchanging information   Points

13 I ... for a drink with my colleagues after work yesterday. I was too tired.
   a go   **b** am going   **c** didn't go   **d** don't go

14 ... going to a restaurant for lunch?
   a Would you like to   **b** How about   **c** Shall we
   d I suggest

15 Please ... to coffee. There are cups on that table.
   a serve yourself   **b** help yourself   **c** take yourself   **d** take

16 "Is there anything you can ... ?" "Yes, the fish is good here."
   a refuse   **b** launch   **c** announce   **d** recommend

17 "What ... products does you company produce?" "We make trainers."
   a kind of   **b** art   **c** for   **d** art of

18 ... some coffee? It'll be ready in a minute.
   a Did you want   **b** Would you like   **c** Please help yourself to
   d Would you care

19 May I ... to Jane Smith? She's our new sales director.
   a present you   **b** introduce you   **c** you present
   d you introduce

Products & processes   Points

20 We have a market ... of 10% in Europe. Our products are selling well there.
   a share   **b** bit   **c** percent   **d** part

21 Most of our goods ... abroad.
   a are exported   **b** export   **c** are exporting   **d** exports

22 The documents ... to our office last week.
   a were delivered   **b** delivered   **c** are delivered   **d** deliver

23 First, the components ... from the supplier.
   a is ordered   **b** are ordered   **c** ordered   **d** order

24 Each car should be thoroughly ... before it leaves the factory.
   a look at   **b** check   **c** inspected   **d** proven

25 Our new ad looks ... . I'm very pleased with it.
   a greatly   **b** well   **c** badly   **d** good

Total points: / 25

Progress check 2 — Unit 4–6

Check your English in units 4-6. Look at these questions (1-25) and tick the correct answer (only one is correct). You get one point for each correct solution.

Figures & negotiations

Points

1. We have a wide … . We sell everything from cameras to computers.
   a sales forecast   b market pressure   c payment terms
   d product range
2. Sales … sharply from €100,000 to €200,000 last year.
   a decreased   b decrease   c rose   d rise
3. Sales … last month. They were at the same level as the month before that.
   a fell sharply   b remained stable   c dropped slightly
   d increased sharply
4. … people work in our London office than in our headquarters in Berlin.
   a Few   b Fewer   c Fewest   d Most
5. "What are your … of payment?" "Customers should pay within 30 days."
   a terms   b rebates   c discounts   d ex-works
6. You drive a hard …, but I can accept your offer.
   a workload   b agreement   c meeting   d bargain

Plans & projects

Points

7. We … dinner with a new customer this evening.
   a are going to have   b have   c eat   d will go
8. If my boss … at our meeting tomorrow, we'll buy some new computers.
   a will agree   b agrees   c won't agree   d agreed
9. What … if they don't deliver the computers?
   a did you do   b are you doing   c will you do
   d do you do
10. Could you please … if you think such a change to the schedule is possible?
    a tell   b confirm   c ask   d reply
11. "… the contract to the supplier yet?" "No, but I'll do it soon."
    a Are you going to send   b Are you sending
    c Have you sent   d Do you send
12. … the sales report yet.
    a I haven't read   b I'm not reading   c I've read
    d I'm reading

Meetings & arrangements

Points

13 "I'm sorry I have no time now, but … you back later."
   a I'll call **b** I call **c** I'm calling **d** I called

14 Unfortunately I will have to … the meeting planned for 10th November. The new date is 15th November at 11 am.
   a put forward **b** call **c** postpone **d** move back

15 Our flight … at 5pm. Don't be late getting to the airport.
   a is leaving **b** leaves **c** is travelling **d** travels

16 We can make an appointment for tomorrow. What time would … you?
   a convenient **b** suit **c** fit **d** make

17 Well, I'm afraid I have to … on that one. Maybe we could talk about this again later?
   a disagree **b** agree **c** say no **d** discuss

18 Here is a first draft of the … for our meeting on Thursday. Please let me know if there is anything you would like to add.
   a map **b** plan **c** schedule **d** agenda

Checking & comparing

Points

19 "When will the installation …?" "By the end of May."
   a completing **b** complete **c** completed **d** be completed

20 "What's the … for transporting the goods?" "It's about €50."
   a trial **b** charge **c** invoice **d** delivery

21 My current job isn't as … my last one.
   a interesting as **b** interesting than **c** interesting **d** more interesting

22 "Jane's not in her office. Where's she … ?" "She's visiting a customer."
   a visiting **b** be **c** been **d** gone

23 "How about if we include transportation?" "Yes, that … fair."
   a gets **b** sees **c** sounds **d** hears

24 Our sales figures dropped last year. Sales were … than the year before.
   a good **b** bad **c** worse **d** less

25 "Will this affect our sales in the long-run?" "Not exactly, but we … other options later this week."
   a will discuss **b** won't discuss **c** are going to discuss **d** discuss

Total points: / 25

Progress check 3 | Unit 7-10

Check your English in units 7-10. Look at these questions (1-25) and tick the correct answer (only one is correct). You get one point for each correct solution.

Small talk & conversation

Points

1. John ... in London since 2008.
   a is working **b** worked **c** works **d** has worked
2. I'll have some soup for my starter then steak and chips for my main ... .
   a menu **b** portion **c** course **d** dish
3. ... we had a lot to do, we still went to the trade fair.
   a However **b** Due to **c** Furthermore **d** Although
4. I'm looking forward ... you.
   a to meet **b** meet **c** meeting **d** to meeting
5. "How long ... in Berlin?" "Since 2009."
   a do you live **b** have you been living **c** did you live
   d are you living
6. I don't know what message our boss was trying to ... to us. Did you understand it?
   a get across **b** get to know **c** get **d** get used

Activities & developments

Points

7. We ... her our new offer two days ago.
   a sent **b** send **c** will send **d** have sent
8. ... to the sales rep before we received his new offer.
   a I'd spoken already **b** I'd already spoken
   c I already spoke **d** I've already spoken
9. She ... to China only once this year.
   a travels **b** has been travelling **c** has travelled
   d had travelled
10. The board hasn't ... a budget increase for our department so there's no more money available.
    a risen **b** missed **c** approved **d** met
11. Our ... has increased sharply. We've sold a lot more books than last year.
    a offer **b** turnover **c** interest **d** loan
12. GlobalCoach ... cross-cultural training for more than a decade now.
    a offers **b** is offering **c** offered **d** has been offering

Presentations & reports

Points

13. Our new smartphone ... yet.
    a wasn't launched b didn't launch c hasn't been launched
    d hasn't launched
14. All our products are ... priced. Our competitors' prices are higher.
    a completely b complete c reasonably d reasonable
15. I'd like to ... your attention to our latest project.
    a borrow b draw c pull d push
16. Would you like ... you with the report?
    a I'll help b I help c that I help d me to help
17. As far as the board ..., we can continue with our new investment.
    a has concerned b is concerned c concerns
    d is concerning
18. We have a very good ... . We are known for the good quality of our products and our excellent service.
    a convenient b reputation c awareness d depreciation
19. Management has ... that we change our tier-one supplier. We should research suppliers who offer the same service at a cheaper price.
    a told b recommended c explained d assisted

Situations & consequences

Points

20. I'd ... if you could send me your new price list soon.
    a appreciated b be appreciated c appreciate
    d appreciate it
21. There's ... wrong with my computer. It's not working.
    a anyone b some c anything d something
22. If we coordinated a single strategy for all our branches, it ... give us an advantage.
    a would b will c was d were
23. Our ... suppliers deliver parts directly to us.
    a level one b level two c tier two d tier-one
24. If the supplier ... the quality of his products, we'd think about buying them.
    a improved b improves c would improve
    d will improve
25. ... you decrease your price, we won't place an order with you.
    a In case b Unless c However d Despite

Total points: / 25

Answer key

Unit 1 pages 5–10

1
- A Human Resources (HR)
- B Research and Development (R&D)
- C Purchasing
- D Logistics and Distribution

2
1. does your department do
2. organize
3. are looking
4. are speaking
5. is preparing
6. Do you think
7. don't know
8. is working

3
1. t
2. f The objectives are discussed with management and the project teams.
3. f They are at various locations.
4. f She's working on a project with a supplier in Asia.
5. f The subject of Jemma's report is about a supplier's product range.
6. f Her time management is very good.
7. t
8. f Logan works with suppliers to find opportunities for price reductions.

4
1. developments
2. supply
3. send
4. manufacture
5. put
6. sell
7. coordinating
8. administration

5
1. parent company
2. production facilities
3. customer care department
4. sales rep
5. product range
6. employee reimbursement

6
1. CEO, Chief Executive Officer
2. CFO, Chief Financial Officer
3. CIO, Chief Information Officer
4. COO, Chief Operating Officer
5. CRO, Chief Risk Officer
6. CTO, Chief Technology Officer

7
1. CEO and COO
2. Head of Sales
3. France, UK, Denmark
4. Head of HR
5. technical, administrative
6. Director of Legal Department
7. Brussels
8. Head of Production Department
9. production facilities

8 *Example*:
I am a product manager in a large electronics company. Usually I work at our headquarters in Berlin, but sometimes I travel to other cities in Germany to meet with clients. My job is to answer their questions about our products and to negotiate business partnerships.

9
1. produces
2. are based
3. is divided
4. include
5. are sold
6. are located
7. builds
8. are sent

10
1. Steven Jones
2. Caledonian Hotel, Princes Street, Edinburgh
3. Jack Shrewsbury
4. 0131 334 559779
5. www.jg-goods.co.uk

11
1. Who is Steven Jones leaving a message for?
2. Which hotel is Steven staying at?
3. What would Steven like to do?
4. Where can Ann find the new website?

12
1. What are you responsible for? / What are you in charge of?
2. How do you spell that?
3. Could you please repeat that?
4. I'm afraid I didn't quite catch that.
5. I hope I'm not disturbing you.

Unit 2 pages 11–16

1 1 d, 2 g, 3 b, 4 h, 5 a, 6 f, 7 e, 8 c

2
1. did you do
2. took
3. was
5. was able to
6. joined
7. used to

    9 were
   10 decided
   11 Were you able to
   12 didn't / did not apply
   13 wanted
   14 used to

3 1 He used to work in Toulouse, France.
   2 There were communication problems between the team and the managing director.
   3 She worked at a pharmaceutical company.
   4 It was interesting and she saw the sights of Paris almost every day.
   5 He found it difficult to delegate tasks. And sometimes he chose the wrong team member for a project.
   6 She had a temporary contract.
   7 He only stayed in Toulouse for six months.
   8 He works at a small engineering firm and can cycle to work.

4 1 persuade
   2 degree
   3 launch
   4 budget
   A DEADLINE
   5 delegates
   6 innovative
   7 contract
   8 deal

5 1993: *joined BMW* in Munich; job in *R&D* department
   1998: *member* of team in US, which *developed* car components
   2001: *returned to Munich*; job in *product development*
   2004: got an *MBA* from university
   2006: *set up* Krenz Automotive Components
   2009: *his company hired twenty new engineers*
   2010: *Krenz Automotive moved headquarters from Regensburg to Munich*

6 *Suggested answers:*
   1 What did Steffen Krenz study? / Who studied mechanical engineering?
   2 Which company did Steffen join? / Who joined BMW?
   3 Where was Steffen's team based? / Whose team was based in the US?
   4 How many engineers were hired? / Who was hired?
   5 When did Krenz Automotive become successful? / Who became successful in 2009?

7 *Example:*
   In 1995, I started my first job as an intern in a bank. Then, I studied finance and management at university before graduating in 2000. After that, I worked in the financial sector for several years. Recently, I decided to return to university and study for an MBA.

8 1 paternity leave
   2 public transport
   3 open-plan office
   4 works council
   5 multinational company
   6 environmentally friendly

9 1 be bought; be purchased
   2 was launched; be used
   3 be imported; be produced
   4 be processed; is done

10 Original order: *one thousand K9 components*
   Original delivery date: *31st July*
   Supplier's problem: *fire in factory*
   New delivery date: *delivery next month*
   New offer: *to reduce price by 10%, offer in writing*
   Future orders: *price reduction of 10% for the next two orders*

11 1 t
   2 f Most of the K7 devices were broken or not of the expected quality
   3 t
   4 f The faulty devices still have not been replaced.
   5 t
   6 f Ruth's colleague could not arrange a time for a meeting.
   7 t

12 1 speak to Ms Brown, please
   2 she's not here at the moment
   3 call back later
   4 returning

Unit 3 pages 17–22

1 1 recently
   2 thorough
   3 highly
   4 general
   5 hardly
   6 short
   7 great
   8 quick

72 Answer key

    3 highly   **6** short

2 **1** h, **2** a, **3** g, **4** d, **5** f, **6** c, **7** b, **8** e

3   **1** f Geoff had to take a taxi because his car broke down.
    2 f He had to put his hand luggage in the hold because it was too heavy and too large.
    3 t
    4 f He would like to discuss the price (general conditions).
    5 f They didn't agree on a new price.
    6 t

4   **1** looking   **5** Did you have
    2 Can I take   **6** this is my assistant
    3 please have   **7** Please help yourself
    4 Would you like   **8** mind me asking

5   **1** were driving
    2 didn't go
    3 was crossing
    4 were discussing; interrupted
    5 did not meet; was working
    6 did; do
    7 were; doing

6 **1** b, **2** a, **3** b, **4** b, **5** a

7 **1** d, **2** g, **3** h, **4** a, **5** b, **6** e, **7** f, **8** c

8 *Suggested answer:*
Dear Anna,

Thank you for your email dated __.__.__. I have some questions about your visit. Could you please give me your flight details: date and time of arrival? If you like, I can send a driver to pick you up from the airport. In addition, I can also arrange hotel accommodation for you if necessary. Could you also please let me know if you would like to go on a company tour? It would make your visit more interesting, and I'm sure it would be a good way to learn more about the company.

I look forward to hearing from you.

Best regards,

9 *Example:*
    A: How about if we go to my favourite Italian restaurant, La Trattoria?
    B: That would be great.
    A: Good, it's a really nice place. It's located in a lovely area right in the old city centre, and they do great antipasti. The service is also very good, and the dessert is fantastic. I can really recommend it.
    B: That sounds perfect. I love antipasti. So let's go there.

10 **1** launch   **5** instruction
     2 competitors   **6** recommendation
     3 changes   **7** inspected
     4 expect

11 **1** ad agency   **4** safety guidelines
     2 skilled worker   **5** protective equipment
     3 key suppliers

12 **1** Have you ever tried Thai food?
     2 What kind of sports do you like to play?
     3 Do you spend a lot of time outdoors?
     4 What's life like in London?
     5 I think Paris is well worth a visit.
     6 I can really recommend this local speciality.

Unit 4 pages 23-28

1 A He is going to eat his steak.
    B She is going to make a telephone call.
    C He is going to give a presentation.
    D She is going to sign a contract.

2 *Example:*
I'm going to meet an old school friend for lunch at my favourite restaurant.
I'm going to talk to my boss about the new project.
I'm going to go on a business trip. I've already bought the train ticket.

3 **1** will not / won't increase
    2 will not / won't go
    3 will/'ll have to
    4 will/'ll contact
    5 will/'ll make

4 **1** b, **2** c, **3** d, **4** a

5

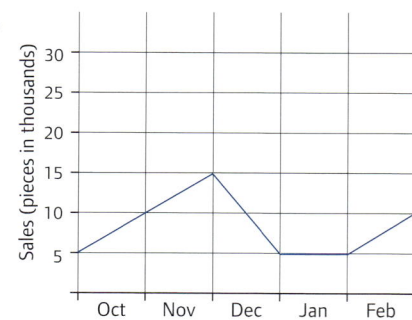

6
1. will be changed
2. will be accepted
3. will/'ll be told
4. will be called
5. will; be trained
6. will/'ll be given
7. will not / won't be delivered
8. will not / won't be informed

7
1. Andrew wants to reorganize work schedules.
2. The reason the company is under pressure is that management brought schedules for the Luxus production line forward.
3. He wants to change to a three-shift system for the next few months, including night shifts.
4. She can't imagine the staff agreeing to this.
5. Staff will be paid double the amount per hour.
6. She can inform Andrew after her meeting – at around 1 pm on Tuesday.

8
1. move on to
2. you feel
3. Sorry to interrupt
4. afraid; have to
5. you mean
6. Are you saying

9
1. f Susan had to postpone the Luxus production line meeting.
2. t
3. t
4. f Management wants to reduce the testing phase from six to three months.
5. f The competitors are behind Premier Dairies in developing their own luxury dairy brands, but they are developing luxury dairy brands.
6. t

10
1. high-end product
2. market pressure
3. premium price
4. machine operators
5. contact details
6. back-up plan

11 Caller: **John K**e**r**ouac
Company: Phonefine
Order: **75** calendars
Product number: EA**387**GH
Order: five camera stands
Order number: JH910D**Q**
Delivery date: August **30**th

12
1. ship
2. invoice
3. charge
4. prediction
5. due
6. current
7. timeline
8. intention
9. stone

A SCHEDULES

13
1. remain stable
2. drop sharply
3. peaked
4. I will/I'll be in touch / I will/I'll let you know
5. be completed by the

Unit 5 pages 29-34

1
1. have
2. will let
3. don't reduce
4. 'll call
5. offer
6. increase
7. 'll speak

2
1. t
2. t
3. t
4. f It is available for only one month (four weeks).
5. f The delivery is free.
6. f The company also has a number of shops.

3
1. … the discount in the new offer for new customers is 15%. The discount for Scopicon is only 5%.
2. … placed their original order.
3. … other Scopicon branches wish to buy fitness machines too.
4. … the other Scopicon branches.

4
1. you what
2. come on
3. may be able
4. How about
5. sound
6. fair

74 Answer key

5 1 older 2 worse 3 more careful

6 1 most successful 5 more expensive
  2 larger 6 highest
  3 busier 7 as strong as
  4 less

7 1 t
  2 f The company did not hire new staff.
  3 f He thinks management should listen to staff.
  4 f He used to work for a legal firm.
  5 f Staff could take extra days off work after completing projects.

8 *Example:*
In my free time, I play guitar in a band with my friends. It's great fun, but to be honest we're not so good. I like it because I can relax and forget about work. I also go walking in the hills near my home. It keeps me fit, and I love the fresh air. I think I have quite a good work-life balance.

9 1 include 4 advance 7 depends
  2 ex-works 5 delivery
  3 terms 6 offer

10 1 bulk discount 4 bank transfer
  2 order form 5 account number
  3 company policy 6 transport costs

11 1 We are the smallest department in the company, but we have the biggest turnover.
  2 Their turnover is worse than ours.
  3 We are one of the most successful companies in this market.
  4 The negotiations were not as difficult as we thought they would be.
  5 Employees who do sport have less stress and find it easier to concentrate.

Unit 6 pages 35–40

1 A Have you ever missed a flight?
  B Have you ever had a meeting in a super-modern conference room?
  C Have you ever been to Birmingham?
  D Have you used the new photocopier yet?

2 1 f She has been at DPN for about eight months.
  2 t
  3 f They have spoken to female students at school.
  4 t
  5 t
  6 t
  7 f He advised her to study engineering.

3 1 Well, actually I've been at the company for about eight months.
  2 You've also established a programme at DPN.
  3 What are you doing to achieve this?
  4 There has been a lot of interest.

4 1 've/have chosen 4 has developed
  2 has come 5 's/has agreed
  3 's/has lead

5 1 did you join 5 haven't / have not stayed
  2 Have; been
  3 's/has gone 6 didn't / did not apply
  4 Have; read

6 *Example:*
The most interesting place I've been to is Paris. I went there about a year ago with some friends. I found the museums and galleries very interesting because we saw many beautiful pictures, which were painted by artists such as van Gogh, Monet etc. The cafés and restaurants are also good. It can be quite expensive there but the food and wine are really excellent.

7 1 Because it will give them time to get new offers from different suppliers.
  2 Because she is meeting her head of department at that time.
  3 He will tell Bill that he will talk to Bill's competitors. That way, Bill might make them a better offer.
  4 David is going to write the agenda.

8 1 does; leave 4 does; arrive
  2 are meeting 5 are; doing
  3 am picking up

9 1 I was wondering if we could make an appointment to discuss our new marketing campaign? Would tomorrow morning at 10 am suit you?
2 Let me see … no, unfortunately that time is inconvenient.
3 That's a shame. Well … how about 12 o'clock on Wednesday?
4 Yes, that would suit me. But my boss may want to see me on Wednesday, and I can't say when exactly.
5 OK, but shall we pencil it in anyway? Maybe you could tell me later today what your boss wants to do?
6 Yes, that should work out. I'll be able to confirm our appointment after I have spoken to him.
7 Fine. See you later.
8 Yes, bye.

10 *Suggested answer:*
Dear Kathy,

We would like to hold a seminar on presentations from Monday, 04.08. to Wednesday, 06.08. Could you please inform me if a seminar room for ten people is available at your hotel for these dates? I would also like to know how much you charge for such seminar rooms. Could you please get in touch with me as soon as possible because I have to finalize the arrangements for this seminar soon?

Kind regards,

11 1 follow-up questions 4 plant manager
2 breakfast meeting 5 data projector
3 voicemail message

12 1 fair 5 value
2 convince 6 confirm
3 inconvenience 7 apologize
4 adaptable 8 succeed
A FINALIZE

13 1 b, 2 a, 3 a, 4 b

Unit 7 pages 41-46

1 1 hasn't / has not sent
2 's/has presented
3 hasn't / has not finished
4 hasn't / has not confirmed

2 1 haven't talked
2 for
3 've/have spent
4 've/have; had
5 Have you decided
6 haven't / have not received
7 've/have been
8 since

3 1 It has increased by 12% (over the first six month of this year).
2 They company needs capital to establish new offices in Cardiff.
3 They pay back around £11,000 every month.
4 The interest rate for mortgages is 3.5%.
5 Because new partners may have different opinions about their plans for the future.
6 Because it will give the banks a good impression. They will see that Sarah and John are serious about their plans.

4 1 established 6 discussed
2 has increased 7 went
3 Have; spoken 8 've/have done
4 've/have had
5 haven't / have not made

5 simple past: four years ago; last week
present perfect: since then; yet; so far; yet; recently

6 1 Well, that was a good meeting.
2 Yes, it was. I'm afraid I'll have to go now though – my flight leaves in two hours.
3 Would you like me to call you a taxi?
4 No, thanks. I think I'll take the underground.
5 Well, it's been good seeing you again. Give my regards to Sonja when you see her next.
6 Sure, I'll tell her you said hello. And thanks again for lunch.
7 That's fine. So … have a good trip home and keep in touch.
8 I will, Tessa. Thanks a lot. Bye.
9 Thank you. Bye.

7 *Example:*
The best hotel I've stayed at was in the countryside in Yorkshire near Leeds. It was family owned, the people certainly knew how to look after guests, and I liked it because of the friendly atmosphere. The food in the restaurant was great too. It was all cooked by the hotel owners themselves!

8
1 actually
2 I'm sorry to say that
3 I'm very sorry
4 Let me take
5 I'm really sorry
6 Unfortunately
7 How about
8 I'm afraid

9
1 someone
2 any
3 anything
4 anywhere
5 any
6 Something
7 some

10
1 It cooperated with an American company, Selby.
2 The company's competitors have reduced the prices on their products by 10%, and the company had some problems with distribution in the American market.
3 Because of an innovative marketing campaign and excellent customer service.
4 In her opinion, the company's marketing campaign is becoming a little old-fashioned.

11
1 I'd like to tell
2 will take about
3 mind; at the end
4 draw your attention to
5 let's now move
6 what about

12
1 participants
2 mortgage
3 cons
4 purpose
A PROPOSAL
5 kick-off
6 interest
7 branches
8 virtual

13
1 How long have you had your office?
2 Let me take your coat.
3 Please give my regards to Sarah.
4 Could I have a glass of wine, please?
5 Feel free to ask questions.

Unit 8 pages 47-52

1
1 forthcoming
2 display stands
3 warehouse
4 giveaways
5 benefits
6 retailers
7 substantial

2
1 trial; of their outlets
2 environmentally-friendly products
3 high-quality eco products
4 new ingredients
5 established
6 any future orders from the UK
7 too expensive

3
1 such as
2 however
3 due to
4 As a result
5 In addition
6 because
7 Although

4
1 b badly designed
2 c clearly seen
3 a highly interesting
4 d warmly welcomed

5
1 It was quite difficult to solve the problem.
2 It wasn't easy to respond to her request.
3 It has been almost impossible to deal with that customer.
4 It was simple to operate our new machines.

6
1 hadn't / had not taken
2 had; called
3 had sent
4 Had; started

7
1 outlined
2 told
3 had given
4 knew
5 invited
6 asked
7 had brought
8 hadn't thought
9 promised
10 returned
11 found
12 had sent

8 1 e, **2** g, **3** c, **4** b, **5** f, **6** d, **7** a, **8** h

9
1 There is not much room in the back of the car (for bags etc).
2 It costs £25,000 (€29,000).
3 The car is quite small so there shouldn't be any parking problems.

4 Marketing can improve customer awareness. They must convince people of the benefits of the technology.
5 The main drawback is the distance that can be driven. You can't drive very far (only about 95 miles) until the batteries are empty.
6 If European companies are too slow, they might miss a very large business opportunity because companies in the Far East are working on the technology.

10 1 f The report was requested by the CEO, Juan de Cusa.
2 f The meeting was held at the headquarters in Berlin.
3 t
4 f On average, they receive €200 per month.
5 t
6 t
7 t
8 f It is recommended to lease the cars.

11 *Example:*
I work for a bank and one product we have is an interesting personal loan. The conditions are very good. The top two benefits of this product are its low interest rate and the fact that customers can decide what they want to use it for. They can also decide how long the loan should last. This could be from two to five years.

12 1 solar panels 4 sales performance
2 electric car 5 customer ratings
3 extra features

13 1 We've / We have made sure that
2 I'd / I would appreciate it
3 actually quite reasonably
4 Although; as many visitors

Unit 9 pages 53–58

1 1 for a few days 5 settled into
2 at a seminar 6 be fine
3 What kind of 7 compared to
4 looking forward to

2 1 Some of the employees in Glasgow will be relocated to the new plant in Bucharest.
2 Romania has been offering financial support to foreign companies for the last five years. The company will save about 15% of the initial costs.
3 They will show the new Romanian employees how to operate and repair the machines.
4 The technicians have been preparing for the project for about a week.
5 She has been thinking about a cross-cultural training for the employees.
6 He should get in touch with a company which specializes in training staff relocating to Eastern Europe.

3 1 relocating some technical employees
2 money over time
3 how to operate and repair
4 the same type
5 attracting foreign companies
6 cross-cultural training

4 1 f The CEO sent the email because he wants to thank staff for being so flexible, especially regarding the transfer of some of the technical staff to Romania.
2 f Cullen has been successful with many different products. First, it produced mechanical devices that were used in telephones. Since the 1950s, Cullen has also been producing mechanical parts for cameras.
3 t
4 t

5 1 has been offering 4 has become clear
2 has made 5 have achieved
3 have discussed 6 have been adding

6 1 order 5 here's
2 recommend 6 starter
3 kind 7 main
4 speciality

7 1 She didn't expect me to go for lunch with the customer.
2 Would you like me to order some drinks for you?
3 They warned me not to eat the local food.

4 I advise you not to talk about politics or religion during lunch.

8 1 f The order number is 231TS.
2 f A number of chairs in the delivery are damaged.
3 t
4 f The shipping department of James' company will collect the damaged chairs.

9 1 to hear that
2 has gone wrong
3 deal with this
4 apologize; inconvenience

10 1 apologize
2 in touch
3 Regarding
4 dissatisfied
5 promise
6 avoid

11 *Example:*
I had to complain about a computer, which I bought last year. I took it home, switched it on but nothing happened. The next day I took it back to the shop and told a member of staff about the problem. He offered me a new computer, but I told him I just wanted my money back – I found it all really annoying.

12 1 corporate language
2 company values
3 management style
4 dress code
5 shipping department
6 competitive prices
7 career advancement

13 1 a, **2** b, **3** a, **4** b

Unit 10 pages 59-64

1 1 Whenever a customer orders a product, our **purchasing department** places an order for the necessary components with the supplier.
2 Then, the supplier sends these components to our **warehouse**.
3 After that, the components are assembled in the production process to make the **final product**.
4 It is then either put into **storage** or transported straight to the wholesaler.
5 The wholesaler delivers this product to the **retailer**.
6 Finally, the **end customer** can purchase the final product from the retailer.

2 1 They were created about one year ago.
2 There would be advantages regarding supplier selection, quality, price and delivery schedules.
3 Because for any project, the people involved must be able to see the benefits for the project to be successful.
4 Steffi and her team could visit the purchasing departments and carry out some workshops.
5 A purchaser's handbook should be published on the intranet.

3 1 would, **2** won't, **3** did, **4** didn't

4 1 d, **2** a, **3** b, **4** f, **5** e, **6** c

5 1 increased, wouldn't have
2 approved, could improve
3 were/was, would speak
4 rose, could pay
5 would happen, went
6 would; do, cancelled

6 1 f There are only enough storage devices in stock for the next three weeks.
2 f Both companies sell their products at the standard retail price.
3 f Kostov could supply storage devices quickly.
4 t

7 1 will run out
2 could provide
3 wanted
4 didn't/did not have

8 1 cutbacks
2 progress
3 responsible
4 over
5 SWOT
6 investment
7 operating
A APPROVE

9 1 Unless
2 in case
3 in case
4 unless
5 in case
6 unless

10 1 He has reached CEF level B1.
2 They answer in German and not in English.

3 Staff can use web-based training on their computers at work and at home.
4 They are discussing whether the staff can use the training during work time.
5 He would like to do a part-time course in sales and marketing at London University.
6 The company might be able to help him with the costs for this course.

11 *Example:*
My company plans to set up an office in Shanghai so I would like to learn some Chinese. I think it would be an advantage if I could say a few simple phrases in Chinese because it would make a good impression. The cultural aspects would also be interesting. That's why I have decided to take part in a weekend seminar in Chinese for Beginners.

12 1 distribution agent
2 standard components
3 sales statistics
4 tight budget
5 unreasonable request
6 back-up plan

13 A: If we don't improve our delivery times, our customers will cancel their orders.
B: What would you suggest?
A: Our current supplier causes all the problems. If he can't meet the deadlines, we will have to look for somebody else.
B: You're right. We need a solution in order not to lose any customers to our competitors.

Progress Check 1 Unit 1-3

Company organisation & responsibilities
1 a, **2** b, **3** d, **4** a, **5** b, **6** a

Personal information
7 b, **8** d, **9** c, **10** d, **11** d, **12** a

Socializing & exchanging information
13 c, **14** b, **15** b, **16** d, **17** a, **18** b, **19** b

Products & processes
20 a, **21** a, **22** a, **23** b, **24** c, **25** d

Progress Check 2 Unit 4-6

Figures & negotiations
1 d, **2** c, **3** b, **4** b, **5** a, **6** d

Plans & projects
7 a, **8** b, **9** c, **10** b, **11** c, **12** a

Meetings & arrangements
13 a, **14** c, **15** b, **16** b, **17** a, **18** d

Checking & comparing
19 d, **20** b, **21** a, **22** d, **23** c, **24** c, **25** a

Progress Check 3 Unit 7-10

Small talk & conversation
1 d, **2** c, **3** d, **4** d, **5** b, **6** a

Activities & developments
7 a, **8** b, **9** c, **10** c, **11** b, **12** d

Presentations & reports
13 c, **14** c, **15** b, **16** d, **17** b, **18** b, **19** b

Situations & consequences
20 d, **21** d, **22** a, **23** a, **24** a, **25** b

Transcripts

Unit 1

Exercise 3

R = Roger, J = Jürgen

R: Thanks for taking the time, Jürgen, for this short interview. I really appreciate it.
J: Oh, don't mention it. I think your idea of writing an article about Logan and its employees is important, particularly following the merger. So … what would you like to know?
R: Well, as you are the head of the purchasing department, I'd like to know how you see the job of a purchaser – a member of your team.
J: Actually, the job of a purchaser is quite demanding. We're responsible for a lot! For example, we have to meet deadlines, and sometimes the time available to complete new projects can be quite short, say two to three months. What's more, any new contract with suppliers must save Logan money, so the objectives are agreed on between management and project teams at our headquarters beforehand.
R: I see. Em, so how do members of your department deal with these tight schedules?
J: We have some training seminars on time management at various locations within the group. It really is a question of prioritizing the work. Some employees are better at that than others. A good example is Jemma Thompson, who is coordinating business with a new supplier in Asia as we speak. She's preparing a report for me now about its product range. Her diary is full of appointments, but she certainly knows how to plan her time.
R: Yes, but your team must put in a lot of hours.
J: Well, it's not really as bad as it sounds. You know, at Logan we have flexitime, which means staff can have some time off work after projects have been completed. In fact, I'm even thinking of going home early today as I've got no meetings this afternoon.
R: Right. So what's the biggest project you're working on at the moment?
J: That's the one Jemma is coordinating. To be honest, most of our projects are pretty big. But the basic message is the same for all our partners. I'm sure you know that we inform suppliers that our objective is to reduce the prices on all equipment we buy. As production costs are higher in Europe than elsewhere, we're looking to Asia to find a number of good suppliers who can offer us what we want. However, it's important to stress that we work together with these suppliers; we don't just say, "Reduce your prices … now!" No … we work with them to see where we can find opportunities for reductions. So it really is a team effort between ourselves and our partners.
R: That must be interesting work. But what about the question of quality? I mean in the last few months …

Exercise 7

As you can see, at the top of the diagram there's the Board of Directors, which is headed by Jane Seymour. Unusually for most companies, she is both CEO and COO, which is a tradition here. Reporting to the board, we have four departments, each responsible for one business area. John Brown heads the sales department, which is active in three countries – France, the UK and Denmark. Germany is a country we'd like to do business in, but we're still at the planning stage. HR is headed by Richard Blake, who's responsible for all technical and administrative staff. Next to HR, you can see the legal department which is actually based in Brussels and not here in London. Anna Lenoir is the director. Finally, on the right we have Linda Crolla. She was head of R&D but now leads the production department and is responsible for our four production facilities. Now, I'd like to explain that each of these departments reports to the Board on a quarterly basis and …

4 **Exercise 10**
Good morning, Ann. This is Steven Jones. I hope you're well and work isn't too demanding. I'm in Edinburgh at the moment and I'd like to come and visit you to present our new product range. I'm staying at the Caledonian Hotel on Princes Street. I'd also like to introduce you to our new director, Jack Shrewsbury – that's S-H-R-E-W-S-B-U-R-Y. Could you please call me back on o-one-three-one-double three-four-double five-nine-double seven-nine? Oh, and by the way, do take a look at our new website – it looks pretty good. You'll find it under www.jg-goods.co.uk. I'm sure you'll like it. Speak to you soon. Bye!

Unit 2

5 **Exercise 3**
A = Anna, P = Peter
A: … globalized environment.
P: Yes, that's right. International experience is important these days. I was actually based in France for some time. I used to work with a product developer – a small firm of about 20 people – in Toulouse. That was about five years ago but, to be honest, things didn't go very well there. There were a lot of communication problems between the team and the managing director. I felt the company didn't really understand the targets and operations of our main clients and sometimes didn't meet the deadlines. I also had to do a lot of travelling around by car, and the roads were terrible in the mornings. I changed jobs because of all that.
A: Yes, but traffic in the morning is the same everywhere in large cities. Y'know … I also worked in France for a while, in Paris.
P: Oh, really? What was your job?
A: I was in a logistics department at a pharmaceutical company. It was an interesting job, and my office was located in the south of the city, which I quite enjoyed. I normally used public transport and saw the sights of Paris almost everyday.
P: Sounds great.
A: Yes, that was good but the job itself was very demanding. My boss at the time found it difficult to delegate tasks. I mean, he could do it, but sometimes he chose the wrong team member for a project. Job security was also a problem. Unfortunately, I only had a temporary contract.
P: And the company didn't give you a new one.
A: Yeah, that's right. I'm now working in London – also in logistics. One positive thing about my time in France is that I was able to learn quite a lot of French which I can now use at work.
P: Y'know … I wish I could speak French fluently. I'm sorry to say that my Toulouse experience didn't give me the chance, really, because I was only there for about six months.

A: I see. Where are you working now?
P: At a small engineering firm in Amsterdam.
A: That must be nice – the city is a lively place.
P: Yes, it is. And believe it or not I can cycle to work, which is better than driving to work in France. The people there are also very friendly, and I find the atmosphere …

6 Exercise 5

Good afternoon. I'd like to introduce our next speaker, Steffen Krenz, who is managing director and partner of the company Krenz Automotive Components. His talk is about the challenges that suppliers face in the automotive industry. Let me first say a few words about him. After graduating from the University of Aachen in 1993 in mechanical engineering, Steffen joined BMW to work in the R&D department in Munich later that year. Five years later, he was a member of a team based in the US, which developed car components for the American market. Then, in 2001, he returned to Munich to continue his career at BMW as a manager in product development. During that year, he returned to his university studies part-time and he successfully obtained his MBA in 2004. Two years after that, he and a number of business partners decided to 'go it alone' and set up Krenz Automotive Components – one of the most innovative components suppliers in the automotive industry. 2009 was the key year for Steffen and Krenz Automotive. They had so much work they hired twenty new engineers. Krenz Automotive became a very successful company. Then, in 2010, the company moved its headquarters from Regensburg to Munich to be at the centre of the car industry in Bavaria. … Oh sorry, I forgot to mention that Steffen also found time to get married four years before that move. He now lives with his family in the centre of Munich. So … please give him a warm welcome – Steffen Krenz …

7 Exercise 10

R = Ruth, P = Paul
R: Hello, Brown Engineering, Ruth MacDonald speaking.
P: Hi Ruth, it's Paul Hillman here. How are things with you?
R: Just fine. So … what can I do for you?
P: I'm phoning about the one thousand K9 components we ordered.
R: Ah, yes I wanted to …
P: If you remember, our deadline for delivery was 31th July, but we still haven't got them. So can you tell me what the status of the order is? Is there a problem?
R: Yes, yes, I know. I wanted to call you earlier. Em, we received some new information yesterday.
P: OK, what exactly?
R: The supplier we buy the parts from has some problems with production. They say there was a fire in their factory last week.
P: OK … but where does that leave me? Our customers are getting a little annoyed, I can tell you. We can't produce our machines until we get these components. Do you think the supplier can deliver them anytime soon?
R: Well, to be honest, they say next month.
P: What! You know as well as I do that's totally unacce …
R: Paul, I have a suggestion.

P: OK ... I'm listening.
R: I'll reduce the price by 10% if you accept the late delivery.
P: Hm. I can see you're doing your best to deal with this. I can try to persuade our customers to accept late delivery of our machines. However, I expect this new price reduction to be continued for the next two orders we place with you.
R: Well, I can agree to that – if you agree to the new delivery date for the current order.
P: Well, alright, but could you please put all this in writing and email it to me?
R: Yes, that's a good idea. Look, Paul, I really am sorry about all this.
P: I know, Ruth, but please give me the new offer asap.
R: Yes, of course. Well ... bye for now.
P: Bye.

Unit 3

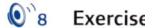

Exercise 3

D = David, G = Geoff, H = Helen

D: Hi there, Geoff. Good to see you again. You're looking well. Can I take your coat?
G: Thanks. So ... how are you?
D: I'm fine. Work is good for me. Anyway, please have a seat. Would you like some coffee? It'll be coming in a minute. Did you have a good trip?
G: Not really, actually.
D: Really? Why was that?
G: Well, first of all, my car broke down. When I tried to start the car, nothing happened. So, I had to take a taxi to the airport. At Heathrow airport I had to put my hand luggage in the hold as it was a little too heavy, and airport staff said it was too large. Anyway ...
D: Ah, coffee. Geoff, this is my assistant Helen Li. Helen, this is Geoff Anderson.
G: How do you do, Helen.
H: Pleased to meet you, Geoff.
D: Thanks, Helen. Please help yourself to coffee and biscuits, Geoff. ... What were you saying?
G: There are a lot of rules and regulations about luggage at Heathrow airport.
D: Well, at least you're here now. ... So, Geoff, if you don't mind me asking, what exactly did you want to talk about today?
G: Well, we're thinking of increasing our orders from you a lot and because of that, I'd like to discuss the general conditions.
D: I see. But all this was agreed on at the end of last year.
G: That's true ... but the situation has changed. Your brand is extremely popular with our customers. Our forecast is that sales will increase by around 20%.
D: Well, that's good to know.
G: That means that we would like to increase the number of shoes that we order from you by the same amount. As that is the case, I'd like to know if you could do anything about the price. Our market share is growing in the UK, which is good for both of us.
D: Mmm. Well ... we sell these shoes to you at a very good price. I don't think we could reduce it much further. How sure are you that sales will increase by 20%?
G: Last year, we worked together with a consultant who looked at the British shoe market. We found out that the sports-shoe market in the UK is growing rapidly. Now that doesn't ...

Unit 4

Exercise 5

As you all know, our sales situation could be better at the moment, and we hope it'll get better during this year. As you can see from this graph, there was a positive development from the beginning of October, when we sold five thousand units. This increased steadily to the end of November, when we were able to sell fifteen thousand units – all in all a very good performance. We expected this trend to continue, reaching a target of twenty thousand units sold by the end of last year, but that didn't happen. Instead, one of our main competitors introduced similar products on the market, which affected our success. So, sales peaked at fifteen thousand at the end of November, decreasing sharply back to five thousand by the end of December. Unfortunately, our forecast is that sales will remain at that level until the end of January. However, because we introduced a new marketing strategy and the installation of a new production line, we expect sales to then rise steadily again to ten thousand units sold by the end of February. We are sure that we will reach our target of twenty thousand units sold by July of next year, thanks to a lot of hard work.

Exercise 7

A = Andrew, C = Christine

A: Right ... I'm glad we agree. This new training programme will help staff communicate better with each other and with customers. It's great that the council agrees. So ... let me move on to the next point: work schedules.
C: Yes ... I read that you want to reorganize the current schedule. I don't think the staff will be happy, but go on.
A: Well, I think you read our CEO's email about the new Luxus production line.
C: Of course I did. He said that we need to increase production with the new production line and that our working practices will have to change. I guess that means more hours and, as you know, the staff are already working at their limit.
A: I understand how you feel, Christine, but we need to make sure that we meet our deadlines at the end of the year. I'm sure you know ...
C: Sorry to interrupt, but that is a management problem. The only reason we're under such pressure is because management brought schedules forward for the Luxus production line.
A: Well, I'm afraid I have to disagree on that one. Maybe we could discuss this later? But anyway, we still need to find a way to increase production.
C: Well, what exactly do you mean by changes to work schedules?
A: I mean changing to a three-shift system for the next few months.
C: Wait a minute. Are you saying that includes night shifts?
A: Well ... yes.
C: With respect, I really can't imagine the staff agreeing to this.
A: Christine, I can offer staff extra payment for working nights. Staff will be paid double the amount per hour.
C: Well, that will certainly be an attractive offer for younger members of staff with no family. I can call a meeting and suggest it to the staff.
A: When can you let me know your answer?
C: I can inform you after the meeting – at around 1 pm on Tuesday. But I still don't understand why management didn't inform me sooner. I really find the whole thing ...

Exercise 11

Ja = Jane, Jo = John

Ja: Foto-for-You, good morning. This is Jane speaking.
Jo: Hi there. This is John Kerouac calling from Phonefine in Manchester.
Ja: Hi John. What can I do for you?
Jo: I'd like to place an order with you. Shall I give you the product number?
Ja: Yes, that would be great. But before we go through your order, could you please tell me your name again and the name of your company? I didn't quite catch the names, sorry.
Jo: Sure. It's John Kerouac that's K-E-R-O-U-A-C. The name of the company is Phonefine that's PHONE with PH and then F-I-N-E.
Ja: OK, what can I do for you?
Jo: I'd like to order seventy five calendars. The product number is E-A-three-eight-seven-G-H.
Ja: Right … I've got that.
Jo: I'd also like five camera stands. The order number is J-H-nine-one-zero- D for Delta -Q for Quebec. I'd like to receive everything by the thirtieth of August. Would that be possible?
Ja: Yes, sure. That should be fine.
Jo: Great. Thanks.
Ja: Thank you for calling, John. We'll let you know when we finished processing your order. Have a nice day. Bye for now.

Unit 5

Exercise 3

S = Sigrid, M = Manfred

S: Thanks for coming to see me again to discuss our order. I really appreciate it.
M: Oh, that's no problem. Anyway, how can I help? When you phoned me it seemed to be quite urgent.
S: Yes, it is quite important. As you know, we placed our order for fourteen fitness machines about six weeks ago and delivery is due at the end of next week. However, on Monday, a colleague of mine in England sent me your new brochure and a letter she received describing a new offer made by Athlete Sports for new customers in Europe. This offer is much better than the one we agreed on at the end of our last meeting in which you gave us a discount of only 5%. I'm really surprised about this, to say the least.
M: Ah, I see. You mean the discount of 15% for new customers stated in the letter.
S: Exactly. Now, I realize that you're trying to get new customers, but I think this new discount should also be offered to us as well.
M: Yes, but with respect, you placed your order about six weeks ago. Our new offer is for this month only.
S: True, but we told you our budget is tight. And we feel that Athlete Sports wasn't exactly open with the conditions. Our order was only just outside the time-period of your new campaign.
M: Well, I'll tell you what. I can give you a new discount of 10%.
S: Oh, come on Manfred. You can give us 15%, I'm sure. You're going to have to …

M: Wait a minute. Let's look at your total order. If you increase the number of items, I may be able to give you a bigger discount.
S: I was just coming to that. Other Scopicon branches informed us last week that they're also interested in buying fitness machines, which means we can do something about the total number of units of equipment. How about if we increase the number to twenty?
M: You mean you want a 15% discount on a new order of twenty machines?
S: Yes, that's right. How does that sound?
M: That sounds fair. OK, Sigrid. I can understand that you feel we should offer you 15% because of our campaign for new customers. If you cancel the original order and make a new one for twenty fitness machines, I'll make sure you get what you want. I'll also give you free delivery to the other branches.
S: And you'll still throw in mats and hand weights for free?
M: Yes, yes, I can still do that.
S: Good. That's great, Manfred. It looks like we have a deal.

🔊 13 Exercise 7

L = Lorraine, P = Paul

L: Yes, the food is good here. Not like my last company. It was really bad there.
P: Yes, eating well is important. I quite like the canteen here. Another good thing about working here is the new fitness room. I used it for the first time yesterday.
L: Did you? I'll have to try it out soon. Y'know … I must say there really is a good working atmosphere here, a lot better than the company I was at before.
P: Really? Why was that?
L: There was a management problem. My job was in a consultant's office, but the problem was that the directors didn't think that a good work-life balance or looking after their employees' health was very important. We were all working around fifty hours per week; sometimes we had to work at weekends.
P: Wow, that's quite a lot! Didn't management do anything to improve the situation?
L: Well, there were one or two activities for staff. Some weekend seminars were arranged on time management, but, to be honest, they didn't really help. They really needed to hire more people so that staff could reduce their working hours.
P: Which they didn't do.
L: No, I'm sorry to say they didn't.
P: Y'know … I think what's really important in a company is that management is ready to listen to staff. Most people work hard and that should be balanced by a healthy life outside the firm. People should have enough time for their own private interests and their families. Management has to give this issue priority.
L: I quite agree. That certainly wasn't the case at the consultant's office. Managers never had time for the staff, so it was not surprising that the staff felt unhappy.
P: Actually, my last employer was quite good at looking after staff.
L: You were at a legal firm, weren't you?
P: Yes, that's right. Management there used to speak to each individual member of staff regularly to find out their opinions on a number of different issues – stress levels, working hours, that sort of thing.
L: Sounds good, but did they do anything about the problems after the discussions?

P: Well, they tried to. There were some extra days that staff could take off work after completing projects, but the main thing was that management listened to their staff.
L: Yes, that's really important. I'm really glad that the relationship between management and staff at our company is so good …

Unit 6

14 Exercise 2

J = Journalist, A = Aysun

J: So, let's welcome our next guest, Aysun Greenfield. Aysun, it's good to have you on the programme.
A: Hello, it's a pleasure to be here.
J: Aysun, you've been at DPN in Dortmund as Head of R&D for around three months now and …
A: Well, actually I've been at the company for about eight months to be exact.
J: Oh, yes. Sorry, my mistake. Anyway, in addition to your YouTube channel called 'Breaking the Glass Ceiling', you've also established a programme at DPN to develop the careers of women at your company. It is obvious that this is very important to you.
A: Yes, it is. I think the opportunities for young women – particularly those who have studied engineering – must be improved. When they come to any company in Europe, their chances of reaching a management position are small. I want to change this, that's why I started this programme at DPN. But, to be honest, that's only part of the challenge. If we inform young women about the career opportunities in engineering, more of them might decide to study engineering at university. In my opinion, the number of female engineers working in Europe must be increased.
J: Right. What are you doing to achieve this? Have you visited any schools?
A: Yes, we have visited schools at least in Dortmund and nearby cities to speak to female students. And I must say there has been a lot of interest.
J: That's good to hear. And what about DPN? When women join the company, how do you look after them?
A: I speak to them and give them advice on a number of topics. I ask them to be open about their problems at DPN – issues such as networking, communication with management and that sort of thing. If there're any issues that I can help them with, I'll do that. I also inform them about additional qualifications they may need if they want to get a higher position within the company. I've found that this programme is really appreciated by female employees.
J: That sounds really interesting. But what about you? Why did you decide to become an engineer?
A: That's a good question. When I was in my final year at school, I actually wanted to study medicine. But I changed my mind after a teacher of mine informed me about the opportunities in engineering. He also told me how rewarding and challenging a career in this field could be.
J: So your teacher did the same as you're doing now – giving advice to young women who are thinking about studying engineering.
A: You know … I've never thought about it in that way but, yes, I suppose you're right. My old teacher probably gave me the idea.

Exercise 7

L = Lana, D = David

L: Hello, Lana Martin speaking.
D: Hi Lana, it's David here. How are things?
L: Just great. I've just got back from my trip to India.
D: I'm glad you're back Lana, because we're going to have to change our plans regarding our project. I'd like to bring the meeting with our main supplier, Bill Watson, forward by three weeks.
L: OK ... but why's that?
D: I think it'll give us time to get new offers from different suppliers. I realize that'll mean a bit more work for us over the next month – we may have to look at deadlines again – but it'll give us a better understanding of prices in the market.
L: Right. So ... when should the meeting take place?
D: Well, I've already spoken to Bill, and we've pencilled in an appointment for next Monday, third of March at 10 am? Would that be OK for you?
L: I'm afraid I'm taking part in a meeting with our head of department at 10 that day. Could we perhaps start at 11? I'll be available then.
D: Let me check my diary ... em, yes that should be possible. I'll have to call Bill just to check, but it should work out. Anyway, when we meet him, I want to discuss the price and tell Bill that we are going to have meetings with his competitors. That way, he may make us a better offer. I'm looking for a reduction of at least 5%.
L: We'll have to keep our fingers crossed on that one. You know that Bill drives a hard bargain. He's not known for reducing prices.
D: I know. But this time, we'll just have to push him. I'm going to write an agenda for the meeting so that we can use the available time well.

Unit 7

Exercise 3

S = Sarah, J = John

S: I think we should start by looking at our present business situation. It doesn't look too bad in my opinion. In fact, I think we're doing rather well.
J: Yes, it does look good. Turnover's increased by 12% over the first six months of this year, which wasn't expected. Our forecast was only 5%.
S: Yes, but is it enough, John? We still need capital to establish new offices in Cardiff.
J: I know, Sarah, but we can always take some credit. We don't have to depend totally on our turnover. Banks will be more than pleased to lend us the money with sales figures like these.
S: Yes, but we shouldn't forget that we already have a very large loan. Remember, we pay back around £11,000 every month. And our other costs are quite high.
J: I realize that, but interest rates have dropped. They're around 3.5% now. It makes borrowing money quite attractive.
S: Actually John, it's 3.5% for mortgages. Loans for businesses are more expensive. The interest rate for business loans is 6%.
J: Well, what do you think? Should we postpone our plans? We could save money that way.

S: We could, but I still think we should consider a new loan, even with our costs. As we've seen, demand for our products has grown. My feeling is that our revenue will increase, but only if we expand. If we don't, we're not going to reach our targets.
J: That's true but I have another idea to get the necessary finance. How about finding other investors to support our company? They could provide the capital.
S: Em … I'm not so sure about that. We need quite a lot of money and I don't think having new partners is realistic. And anyway, I think we have to make the right decisions for the company. New partners may have different opinions about our plans for the future. They might not like them.
J: You're right there. So, it seems a bank is the best option. I could look around for the best deals.
S: Actually, I think we should go to the banks together to speak to the responsible people for loans. If we both go, it'll give them a good impression. They'll see we're serious about our plans.
J: OK … I like that idea. I'll call some banks straight away to get some appointments.

🔊 17 Exercise 10

T = Tom, S = Sue

T: So, let me now invite our sales director, Sue Jones, to talk about our sales performance. Sue, …
S: Thanks, Tom. Good morning, everybody. As Tom mentioned, I'd like to tell you about our recent sales performance and there are three main points I'd like to make. Firstly, our position in the US market, secondly, our business situation in the European Union and finally our opportunities for the future. My presentation will take about twenty minutes and if you don't mind, I'd like to take questions at the end.
So, I'd like to begin with the US. Four years ago, we were able to make a successful start in the US market thanks to our cooperation with the American company, Selby. However, as you know, this year we've had some problems and we're not reaching our sales targets. There are two main reasons for that. Firstly, our competitors have reduced the prices on their products by about 10% on average, which has had a negative influence on our market share. I'd like to draw your attention to this slide which shows our falling sales figures in the US. Secondly, we've also had some problems with distribution in the American market. We don't seem to be able to deliver our goods to our retail outlets on time at the moment. These two issues will have to be discussed later this afternoon and I'm sure we'll find some solutions.
So, let's now move on to our business situation in Europe. This, I'm happy to say, is much more positive. Sales have risen sharply over the last three years which is explained by our innovative marketing campaign and excellent customer service. Because of that, we have been able to increase our market share in the EU by 15%. However, we still have to be careful here. My own opinion is that our marketing campaign is now three years old and is becoming a little old-fashioned. The time has come to invest more money in advertising so that we can reach new customers with a clear message about the quality of our products. It's something we all have to think about. Remember, our competitors are not wasting time either. A new advertising campaign will also have to be discussed later this afternoon.

So, what about our business opportunities for the future? As we have seen, our position in the US doesn't look so good at the moment, but I think we can change that by looking at a number of factors. Firstly, our distribution can be improved by …

Unit 8

 18 **Exercise 2**

U = Uli, M = Maria

U: Hi Maria. How are things with you? Good I hope.
M: I'm just fine. You sound very happy.
U: I've got a good reason to be. You know that the British eco-supermarket chain, Value It, has just placed a substantial order with us for our detergent, Ecoclean.
M: Yes, I heard about that.
U: Well, when I returned to the office today I heard that we'd got a call from another UK retailer who'd visited our stand at the Natexpo trade fair in Paris. They've placed a trial order for five of their outlets for the same product.
M: Hey, that's great news.
U: Yes, it is. What really convinced them to give Ecoclean a go was the fact that it's produced in an environmentally-sustainable way. Their marketing department plans a campaign focussing on environmentally-friendly products. They think that customers are willing to pay slightly more for high-quality eco products. And compared to other products, Ecoclean is still reasonably priced. I think our sales in the UK market could really increase on the basis of those two orders. The potential is large.
M: That's great. You've done well, Uli. If we can improve our position in the UK, it'll compensate for our disappointing sales in Spain and Portugal. Mmm, actually, I'm glad you called because I just spoke to our production manager, and I'm afraid he mentioned that there are some quality problems with Ecoclean.
U: Oh, no. What sort of problems?
M: It's to do with the new ingredients we've just put into the product. It looks like they sometimes change the colour of the detergent. It's nothing too serious, but it does mean we're going to have to find a solution – and that's going to take time. However, the production department says they need about a week to sort it out.
U: Well, that's not too long. I'm sure they'll be able to solve the problem. My main concern at the moment is to make sure we establish the right sales team for the UK market. Unfortunately, we don't even have one sales rep there.
M: Yes, we really need a sales team to deal with all those new orders from the UK. How do you think we can find the right people?
U: Well, at the moment I think we can deal with any future orders that come from the UK here in Germany, although it might be difficult because of the amount of business we have. It really depends on how the market develops in the UK. But at some point soon, we'll need people who are based there. It's all a question of timing. If we hire people too early, it may be too expensive.
M: Yes, but do you think we should move people from offices in Europe to the UK?

Transcripts 91

Exercise 9

P = Presenter, B = Bill

P: Hello everybody and welcome to the programme. Everyone's talking about electric cars these days, and I'm here to have a look at one that's just come on the market – it's the new Maurice TX. It certainly looks very good, but let's take a look inside. Well, the seats are very comfortable and, from the inside, the TX looks like many of the cars we know today. Unfortunately, there's not much room in the back of the car, so you aren't going to be able to use it for holidays with the children. There isn't enough room for them AND your bags – so you might have to leave the kids at home!
…
I'm now driving down Bayswater Road in London, and I have to say that I'm enjoying the experience. The TX is easy to drive, it moves quickly and it's very quiet. At twenty-five thousand pounds (that's about twenty-nine thousand euros), the car is not really reasonably priced. But if you drive a lot in the city, this is the car for you! It's small, so you won't have any problems parking around town, and the batteries are technologically advanced. You can drive for about ninety-five miles before they run out. Nonetheless, the big question is: will people buy electric cars in the future? I asked Professor Bill Gallagher, an expert from the University of Edinburgh.

P: Very nice to have you on the show, Professor. Thank you for coming. So, Professor, how high will demand be for electric cars in the future?
B: Well, they've certainly made it to the market, and demand will definitely grow. But, to be honest, there are two issues here: price and customer awareness. Manufacturers must convince people of the benefits of this technology. Customer awareness is not that high at the moment.
P: So it's a question of marketing the product.
B: That's right.
P: Do you see any drawbacks with the electric car?
B: Yes, I do. You can't drive very far. Although performance has improved here, the average distance that can be driven until the batteries are empty is about ninety-five miles. But that's not good enough if drivers are going to use the cars over long distances between cities.
P: But the car industry is working on it.
B: Oh, yes. It's investing a lot of money in new technologies, but I'm not sure if the improvements will be available fast enough. European manufacturers will have to be careful because companies in the Far East – in countries such as Japan, Korea and China – are working on this technology. We have to be quicker in Europe in order not to miss this very large business opportunity.
P: OK, but what about North America? If we consider that …

Unit 9

Exercise 2

P = Paula, R = Richard, D = Dave

P: Well, that brings us to the next point on the agenda – relocating some technical employees from our plant in Glasgow to the new one in Bucharest and finding new employees in Romania.

So, what about our business opportunities for the future? As we have seen, our position in the US doesn't look so good at the moment, but I think we can change that by looking at a number of factors. Firstly, our distribution can be improved by …

Unit 8

 Exercise 2

U = Uli, M = Maria

U: Hi Maria. How are things with you? Good I hope.
M: I'm just fine. You sound very happy.
U: I've got a good reason to be. You know that the British eco-supermarket chain, Value It, has just placed a substantial order with us for our detergent, Ecoclean.
M: Yes, I heard about that.
U: Well, when I returned to the office today I heard that we'd got a call from another UK retailer who'd visited our stand at the Natexpo trade fair in Paris. They've placed a trial order for five of their outlets for the same product.
M: Hey, that's great news.
U: Yes, it is. What really convinced them to give Ecoclean a go was the fact that it's produced in an environmentally-sustainable way. Their marketing department plans a campaign focussing on environmentally-friendly products. They think that customers are willing to pay slightly more for high-quality eco products. And compared to other products, Ecoclean is still reasonably priced. I think our sales in the UK market could really increase on the basis of those two orders. The potential is large.
M: That's great. You've done well, Uli. If we can improve our position in the UK, it'll compensate for our disappointing sales in Spain and Portugal. Mmm, actually, I'm glad you called because I just spoke to our production manager, and I'm afraid he mentioned that there are some quality problems with Ecoclean.
U: Oh, no. What sort of problems?
M: It's to do with the new ingredients we've just put into the product. It looks like they sometimes change the colour of the detergent. It's nothing too serious, but it does mean we're going to have to find a solution – and that's going to take time. However, the production department says they need about a week to sort it out.
U: Well, that's not too long. I'm sure they'll be able to solve the problem. My main concern at the moment is to make sure we establish the right sales team for the UK market. Unfortunately, we don't even have one sales rep there.
M: Yes, we really need a sales team to deal with all those new orders from the UK. How do you think we can find the right people?
U: Well, at the moment I think we can deal with any future orders that come from the UK here in Germany, although it might be difficult because of the amount of business we have. It really depends on how the market develops in the UK. But at some point soon, we'll need people who are based there. It's all a question of timing. If we hire people too early, it may be too expensive.
M: Yes, but do you think we should move people from offices in Europe to the UK?

🔊19 **Exercise 9**

P = Presenter, B = Bill

P: Hello everybody and welcome to the programme. Everyone's talking about electric cars these days, and I'm here to have a look at one that's just come on the market – it's the new Maurice TX. It certainly looks very good, but let's take a look inside. Well, the seats are very comfortable and, from the inside, the TX looks like many of the cars we know today. Unfortunately, there's not much room in the back of the car, so you aren't going to be able to use it for holidays with the children. There isn't enough room for them AND your bags – so you might have to leave the kids at home!
…
I'm now driving down Bayswater Road in London, and I have to say that I'm enjoying the experience. The TX is easy to drive, it moves quickly and it's very quiet. At twenty-five thousand pounds (that's about twenty-nine thousand euros), the car is not really reasonably priced. But if you drive a lot in the city, this is the car for you! It's small, so you won't have any problems parking around town, and the batteries are technologically advanced. You can drive for about ninety-five miles before they run out. Nonetheless, the big question is: will people buy electric cars in the future? I asked Professor Bill Gallagher, an expert from the University of Edinburgh.

P: Very nice to have you on the show, Professor. Thank you for coming. So, Professor, how high will demand be for electric cars in the future?
B: Well, they've certainly made it to the market, and demand will definitely grow. But, to be honest, there are two issues here: price and customer awareness. Manufacturers must convince people of the benefits of this technology. Customer awareness is not that high at the moment.
P: So it's a question of marketing the product.
B: That's right.
P: Do you see any drawbacks with the electric car?
B: Yes, I do. You can't drive very far. Although performance has improved here, the average distance that can be driven until the batteries are empty is about ninety-five miles. But that's not good enough if drivers are going to use the cars over long distances between cities.
P: But the car industry is working on it.
B: Oh, yes. It's investing a lot of money in new technologies, but I'm not sure if the improvements will be available fast enough. European manufacturers will have to be careful because companies in the Far East – in countries such as Japan, Korea and China – are working on this technology. We have to be quicker in Europe in order not to miss this very large business opportunity.
P: OK, but what about North America? If we consider that …

Unit 9

🔊20 **Exercise 2**

P = Paula, R = Richard, D = Dave

P: Well, that brings us to the next point on the agenda – relocating some technical employees from our plant in Glasgow to the new one in Bucharest and finding new employees in Romania.

R: What are your thoughts?
P: As we all know, hiring people in Romania is a lot cheaper than in the UK. Plus, Romania has been offering financial support to foreign companies for the last five years. We'll save about 15% of the initial costs that way.
R: Yes, the plant in Bucharest will save the company money over time.
D: That really is a big advantage. But let's come back to the agenda and have a look at our new Romanian workers. What kind of profile should they have?
P: We'll mainly need technical staff, I think. It'll take about six months until the plant is in operation. During that period, our technical staff has been showing the new Romanian employees how to operate and repair the machines. The machines we will use in Romania are the same type as the ones we have been using in Glasgow for the last two years.
R: OK, but how many of our technicians do you want to relocate?
P: There are five in all. We've already spoken to them and they've agreed. They have been preparing for the project for about a week now.
R: Does their preparation include any intercultural or language training?
P: The Romanian workers have been studying English since Romania started attracting foreign companies. And we plan to provide Romanian translators for our British employees.
R: Right. But Paula, how about more diversity training for our people?
P: Yes, I have been thinking about that for quite some time now. I think a cross-cultural training could help us here. It's just not that easy to find a company that provides intercultural team training for employees relocating to Romania.
D: I've heard of a company that might be able to help us. It's based in London and it has been training staff relocating to Eastern Europe for five years. Should I get in touch with them?
P: That sounds interesting. Yes, could you do that, please?
D: OK then, I'll call them straight away and set up a meeting …

🔊 21 Exercise 8

J = James, S = Sophie

J: Office and More, customer care, James Taylor speaking.
S: Good afternoon. This is Sophie Dupont from Lyons Services.
J: Good afternoon. How may I help you?
S: I'm calling about an order that I placed for a consignment of thirty office chairs.
J: Do you have an order number for me, please?
S: Yes, it's 2-3-1-T-S.
J: Thank you. So, let me check the status of the order. Em, yes, they were sent out yesterday. Didn't you receive them?
S: Yes, but that's not the problem. The trouble is that a number of chairs in the delivery are damaged.
J: Oh dear, I'm sorry to hear that. How many are damaged exactly?
S: Well, fifteen. It all is very annoying.
J: Well, obviously something has gone wrong here. We will of course sort this out for you immediately. I'll make sure we send you fifteen new chairs.
S: OK, but I hope you can offer me some sort of compensation.

J: Well, how about if we give you a discount on this order of, say, 5%?
S: OK, that sounds fair.
J: Em, Ms Dupont, about the damaged chairs ... How about if I talk to our shipping department to collect them and deliver the new chairs by express – at no extra charge to you, of course. Does that sound OK?
S: Yes, that sounds good.
J: OK then, I'll deal with this straight away. Thank you so much for calling, Ms Dupont. I apologize again for the inconvenience.
S: Thank you. Bye.
J: Bye.

Unit 10

Exercise 2
S = Steffi, M = Matt, A = Amy
S: The reason I want to talk to you today is because we need to discuss our purchasing guidelines. As you know, the board wants us to make sure that all purchasing departments follow the same guidelines when doing business with tier-one suppliers.
M: But we set up the guidelines at our headquarters about a year ago. Are you saying that no one knows about them?
S: Not at all, but I think they haven't been communicated well to the responsible people. We have to think about the ...
A: Excuse me for interrupting Steffi, but is it really necessary for all purchasing departments to follow the same company guidelines? I mean we have five main locations in Europe. Each office knows its local market well and understands how its suppliers fit into the supply chain.
S: That's true, but we should look at the bigger picture. If we set up a single European strategy, it would give us more advantages regarding supplier selection, quality, price, and delivery schedules. We should look at the long-term benefits rather than short-term profit.
M: Sure, so ... the objective should be to communicate our guidelines to our subsidiaries.
S: Exactly. If we don't do that, we won't get anywhere. Remember, this is a great opportunity to make some large savings for the whole company.
A: What I don't understand though is why we have to convince the people in our subsidiaries about the advantages. It's an order from above and should simply be followed.
S: That is true, but we should consider that for any project, the people involved must be able to see the benefits for it to be successful. That's why it's our job to get the message across.
M: So what should we do, Steffi?
S: Why don't we visit the purchasing departments at each of our European subsidiaries and carry out some workshops. If we did that, there would be a good chance that we'd get the message across.
A: Good idea. Maybe we should also create a purchaser's handbook in case anyone can't take part in the workshops – we could also publish it on our intranet.
M: Yes, then everyone could read it. But what would we do if purchasers didn't follow the guidelines even after all our proposals?

S: Yes, that could be a problem, but I suggest we deal with that as it arises. Now, how are we going to …

23 Exercise 10
L = Lisa, J = James

L: … so, James, all-in-all you've done very well this year and I'm very pleased with your performance. You've even found time to improve your German.
J: Yes, I really liked the course the company offered. The trainer was very good, and when I started I really was a beginner.
L: But I see from your certificate that you've reached CEF level B1.
J: That's right. I still have some difficulties – for example, when I call our offices in Austria, but at least people don't answer me back in English anymore, which is good. I'd like to continue the course and try for B2 level.
L: Well actually, that might not be possible.
J: Oh, that's a shame. May I ask why?
L: I'm afraid there's no budget for language training next year. It's too expensive, but we'd like to try out a new idea. We've just got in touch with a company which offers web-based training.
J: I see, but I think having a teacher is better because he can correct my mistakes, and he knows about my language needs.
L: OK, but have you tried web-based training before?
J: Well no, but all I'm saying is that classroom lessons with a trainer are better.
L: But you could try it out at least.
J: OK, I suppose we could give it a go.
L: The advantage with this idea is that you can use the web-based system using your computer at home and at work.
J: OK, but will I be able to learn this way during work time?
L: We're discussing that issue at the moment, but it seems it should be possible. Anyway, what about other training programmes for next year? What would you like to do?
J: Well, I've been thinking about doing something to develop my knowledge of sales and marketing. There's a part-time course offered by London University that I'm very interested in.
L: That sounds good. Em … perhaps our company could help you with that regarding the costs. We would need to know more about it, though.
J: Well, I could show you what it's all about. I've got a brochure which describes the course in detail.
L: Good idea. I suggest we arrange another meeting for next week to discuss it. By the way, I think this is very good, James. I like to see employees looking for training opportunities. It's good for the member of staff and the company …

Audio-CD – Track list

#	Track	Time
1	Copyright	00:47
Unit 1		
2	ex. 3	02:53
3	ex. 7	01:19
4	ex. 10	01:04
Unit 2		
5	ex. 3	02:43
6	ex. 5	02:06
7	ex. 10	02:17
Unit 3		
8	ex. 3	02:42
Unit 4		
9	ex. 5	01:39
10	ex. 7	02:08
11	ex. 11	01:41
Unit 5		
12	ex. 3	03:00
13	ex. 7	02:45
Unit 6		
14	ex. 2	03:02
15	ex. 7	02:00
Unit 7		
16	ex. 3	02:50
17	ex. 10	03:06
Unit 8		
18	ex. 2	02:51
19	ex. 9	03:05
Unit 9		
20	ex. 2	02:22
21	ex. 8	01:55
Unit 10		
22	ex. 2	02:41
23	ex. 10	02:36
Total running time		**53:48**

Studio: Clarity Studio Berlin

Aufnahmeleitung: Christian Schmitz

Tontechnik: Pascal Thinius

Regie: Christian Schmitz, Anna Batrla

Sprecher/innen: Shaunessy Ashdown, Noémi Besedes, Laura Cameron, Steve Ellery, Mala Ghedia, Murdo MacPhail, Ruth Michaelson, Christian Schmitz, Darren Smith, Brittani Sonnenberg, Kenneth Spiteri, Felix Würgler